the WAVES *of*
HEALING
GLORY

Endorsements

It's been a very dry season since the last great move of God's Spirit worldwide. But it's finally here! Becky teaches from hands-on experience on how to be equipped for the last and greatest *Waves of Healing Glory* in history!

SID ROTH
Host, *It's Supernatural!*

One of the most controversial and misunderstood truths in the Bible is healing and how to receive your manifestation after you have asked. Many people look to other people for their healing instead of reaching out and surrendering to our Lord and Savior Jesus Christ. Becky's book, *The Waves of Healing Glory,* is a book you will want to purchase, read, and share with others. We know that a tsunami is huge and overtakes everything in its path. Get ready for this tsunami of healing that God is bringing to the West! God is willing to heal—and this book helps you receive your healing and minister to others.

MARILYN HICKEY
Marilyn Hickey Ministries

the WAVES *of* HEALING GLORY

Prepare Yourself for the End-Times
Tsunami of Signs, Wonders, Miracles,
and the Greater Works Jesus Promised

BECKY DVORAK

DESTINY IMAGE® PUBLISHERS, INC.

P.O. Box 310, Shippensburg, PA 17257-0310

"Promoting Inspired Lives."

This book and all other Destiny Image and Destiny Image Fiction books are available at Christian bookstores and distributors worldwide.

Cover design by Eileen Rockwell

Interior design by Terry Clifton

For more information on foreign distributors, call 717-532-3040.

Reach us on the Internet: www.destinyimage.com.

ISBN 13 TP: 978-0-7684-5462-8

ISBN 13 eBook: 978-0-7684-5463-5

ISBN 13 HC: 978-0-7684-5465-9

ISBN 13 LP: 978-0-7684-5464-2

For Worldwide Distribution, Printed in the U.S.A.

1 2 3 4 5 6 7 8 / 25 24 23 22 21

Dedication

What could be more meaningful, especially in today's world, than a true friend who stands with you through the thick or thin of life? I have been blessed with a group of people, handpicked by God who qualify as being true friends. Not only do they love God, but they also love me, and demonstrate their love toward me by sacrificing their time to intercede for me personally, for my family, for the Healing and Miracles International ministry, and for the people who receive a healing touch of God's love through the outreach of this ministry.

Whatever the need is, no matter how challenging the situation appears, they hold me up with their prayers of faith. To honor them in return, I have shared various testimonies about these special people throughout this work—I know you will see why I am so grateful to have them in my life.

I am honored to have as my friends: Palma, my ministry assistant and close friend; willing Dexter; supportive Tiffany; bold Monica; encouraging Blanche; caring Terri; gentle Odessa; and sweet Martha.

Acknowledgments

I truly give a big thank you to Destiny Image Publishers for a fantastic job to help me put this message, *The Waves of Healing Glory,* into your hands. And a special thanks to Larry Sparks (publisher), Angela R. Shears (editor), Eileen Rockwell (cover designer), Terry Clifton (page designer), and John Martin (production manager). You are a great team to work with, and I appreciate your professionalism.

Contents

Introduction

It's not the educational aspect of the "how to" lay hands on the sick that creates great miracles. I can effectively train you to do so within a session or two. But what creates great miracles in the natural is birthed deep in the supernatural realm.

Witchdoctors have grabbed hold of my hands and asked me for my power to heal. They have searched my rings, bracelets, and any other thing that might possibly be a trinket of tricks to produce unexplainable miracles. Also, countless numbers of Christians have touched me, even begged me to give them this healing power. God's people have even become angry with me, thinking I was withholding something from them.

And I respond basically the same way to all, "You can have what I have, even more, but you have to surrender to the Messiah—our Lord and Savior—Jesus Christ. And may I be perfectly clear that it's not me or another human being you want to touch—that's idolatry. You need to touch the heart of our God—He's the One you need to grab hold of and not let go."

In this work, *The Waves of Healing Glory*, you will discover the six waves of God that are moving across this earth, plus the counter-waves the enemy is using against the Church. And you will learn the deep secrets in the supernatural realm that will take you to this level of faith or trust in our Redeemer to work through you as He wills in this latter-day tsunami wave of healing glory.

The Waves of Healing Glory was birthed from many years, and still counting, in my studies of the healing Word of God, practical hands-on healing ministry experience, and from a prophetic vision from the Lord. It is a message for now, especially now, to help empower and embolden the Body of Christ to step into this amazing healing wave of glory of tsunami strength to heal our own physical bodies, minds and emotions, and our spiritual beings—and to heal those around us too. And to heal our nations, cities, and communities during these latter days while chaos is breaking out all around us.

Step into this Living Water. It's what you have been waiting for.

1

Tsunami Wave of Healing Glory

Along with reading His will and desire for our health and well-being in the Scriptures, the Lord continues to give me dreams and visions and prophetic utterances about waves being released onto this earth. These prophetic sightings started with the following vision I call, *"A Tsunami Wave of Healing Glory."*

In a vision the Lord showed me on January 7, 2012, a tsunami wave of supernatural healing hitting the Western world. And He said to me, "No longer will people say, 'Why doesn't divine healing manifest here?'"

A wave of divine healing is overtaking the West. Expect to get wet!

But along with this wave will be a strong undertow of unbelief that will try to pull you away. Don't allow satan the liberty to pull you under. Rise to the top and believe.

This wave is different from before. It won't be in isolated locations with pockets of people receiving. This wave will manifest in all places to all people.

Ministers of healing are rising to the top of this wave. Not only will we minister healing, but we also will equip others to ride the wave.

The blind see, the deaf hear, the mute speak, the paralytics walk, incurable diseases are healed, and the dead rise. Unusual types of miracles are also in this wave—and it has arrived at the Western shores.

Don't be afraid of this Living Water. It's what you have been waiting for. This powerful tsunami wave overtakes and heals all who are willing to step in and get wet.[1]

Many are of the mindset that God only heals those who are in poverty-stricken nations. Or the unfortunate ones who don't have access to good medical care. But I ask you, "Is this truth or just hearsay?" It is the latter. We in the Western world have seen how suddenly the richest nations can fall into calamity and financial hardships and share in the same tribulations with the developing nations.

Times are changing, and so too is the earth and its inhabitants. Truly, I say to you that God is not geographical. He goes wherever there is a believing heart, and believing hearts can be found anywhere in the world—in every hemisphere. And the one believing can call out to Him at any given time—morning, noon, or night—and the Lord Himself promises to hear us when we call to Him.

Word of the Lord

The Spirit of the Lord would say to you this day,

> A tsunami wave of healing glory has been released throughout the whole earth. It has begun in the deep and unseen things of My Spirit. It is released for such a time as this, when the eternal powers of darkness and the Light are fighting for the right to claim your eternal destination. You are living in difficult days; My prophets of old forewarned you of these so very long ago.
>
> The healing power of My Spirit has been given to you to combat the vile plagues and pestilence that are being released in waves and overtaking the inhabitants of this world. But I say to you, with just one healing touch, one prophetic word of faith from My people who are called by My name and obey,

> they can literally eradicate the disease and put it in its place—under the submission of the authority that I have given to those who love Me and are called by My name—Yeshua, your Messiah.

Supernatural Powers of Faith Operate When Faith Is Switched On

The point I want to make clear is that manifestations of God's promises are not operative because of the physical location of the individual or regional good fortunes, but are activated when the supernatural powers of faith are switched on. Permit me to share a testimony to bring this opening point home for you.

Joaquin is a physically fit young man and a hard worker; but more importantly, he is a Christian who had been suffering with severe back pain for several years. And no matter how I tried to encourage him to activate his faith in God, he struggled to believe at this point in life. You see, he, like so many of our young people, had strayed for a while from his faith, not long, but long enough to open the door for the enemy, satan, to wreak havoc in his life. Since that time, he has rededicated his life to the Lord, but honestly struggled with his faith that God could forgive him and answer him when he called out to Him.

But then Joaquin had one of those revelation moments, an Aha! Moment of Truth when he got it, and the expressions of his life honestly testified that he actually got it! And I pray the same for you—an Aha! Moment of Truth with this message written for you.

I know Joaquin well—he is our son. At the time of this writing he's 20 years of age, living with his wife, Rose, and their sweet little girl in their home at our "children's home" at the edge of a village in Guatemala, Central America. He had a personal revelation of this truth of faith just the other day. Now, allow me to set the stage for you a little more so that you too can receive the same revelation, that God is waiting for you, whoever you are and wherever you are, to call out to Him and turn on your faith.

Most would think Joaquin had an upper edge on the situation, after all he did grow up with a prophetess and healing evangelist for his mom. And yes, he was privy to hear firsthand testimonies of amazing miracles, and even was a witness to a number of them; but even still, life has a way of clouding our spiritual eyes. And furthermore, no longer did his missionary parents live in the upper level above him and his family. In fact, Mom and Dad moved to the United States, while he lives in Guatemala. So no longer does he have the convenience of running upstairs for healing prayer. He has to activate his own faith in the Great Healer—Jesus Himself.

And he did just that—Joaquin activated his faith for his own healing. One morning I received a phone call from him testifying how he received his manifested healing for his back. The day before, he was standing in line at the bank to deposit some money. He saw an old friend and found out she was working in the medical field. He asked if someone where she worked could check out his back and recommend a remedy for the intense pain he had been suffering from for way too long.

As they conversed, he realized it would cost him a lot more money than he had and there would be no guarantee of healing. At that very moment, the words of his mom came rushing to his mind to "Trust God, believe and receive Yeshua's healing power." Right then he pray in faith believing he was healed—and he was. He tested it out all day long, and the next morning called me to testify. He said with joy, "Mom, write it down that on May 5, 2020, I received my healing for my back."

I share all of this because you, the reader of this message, might be able to come up with reasons why you think others have the upper edge to access God's miraculous healing power—because of where they live, or who they live with, or who they know. But I'm telling you, there comes a point in each of our lives when we all have to call upon the name of the Lord for ourselves and trust in His healing grace for our own bodies, *and* for those He has entrusted in our care.

As a young husband, Joaquin had to activate this miracle-working power for his wife and their second child who at the time of this writing is expected to arrive soon. Several months ago, we received an emergency phone call from Joaquin saying that Rose was expecting a child, but was in the hospital under medical supervision because she was bleeding heavily, and the reports were bad. A doctor told them to abort the baby, but Joaquin stood his ground and rebuked the head doctor and firmly said, "No!" They would never do such a thing.

Instead of following ungodly counsel of the medical profession, Joaquin called us and we all prayed together in faith and believed and confessed the healing promises in God's Word over Rose and the unborn baby. A few days later, she was released from the hospital as if nothing had ever happened. The medical professionals witnessed a miracle in a hopeless situation.

We must admit that these are troubling times for us all. And perhaps, like Joaquin and Rose, you need God to deliver you from trouble. Take up strength with these words found in Psalm 50:15 where our faithful God reaches out to us in comfort and says, *"Call upon Me in the day of trouble; I will deliver you, and you shall glorify Me."*

Obviously, it is God's will that we are placed on earth, for such times as these, in the midst of distressing times brought on by our enemy—the devil. Not so that we are crushed by these troubling events, but so that we actuate the supernatural power of our faith and display a host of miraculous signs and wonders that bring glory to our Deliverer and Savior—Yeshua.

Now that we see how God expects His people, no matter who we are or where we are or who we know, to switch on the supernatural power of our faith for our physical bodies and for those He has entrusted us with, let's move into a supernatural tsunami wave of healing glory that is breaking forth all around us.

A Tsunami Wave of Healing

Could it be that God is asking all of His disciples like Joaquin and you and me to release this marvelous healing power to those all around us? I believe so; in fact, I know this to be true. I read His will and desire for us in the Scriptures that He wants us to be well, and that we use His healing power to minister to those in need.

> *Beloved, I pray that **you may prosper in all things and be in health,** just as your soul prospers* (3 John 1:2).
>
> *Confess your sins to each other and **pray for each other that you may be healed.** The prayer of a righteous person is powerful and effective* (James 5:16 NIV).

You see, this tsunami wave of healing glory is not just a few isolated cases of healing happening here and there—it is a saturation of healing power for those who want it. If you want to step into this supernatural tsunami wave of healing glory, let's move ahead.

Activate God's Healing Power in Developed Nations Too

You read Joaquin's personal healing testimony of his back and how he activated faith for the life of his wife and unborn baby, but for some reason you may think to yourself, *Well, Joaquin is in Guatemala, which is a developing nation. So he somehow has a spiritual advantage to activate God's healing power because, after all, his options are limited. He has to go to God.* Hmmm, allow me to share with you a recent healing testimony from the Western world, a developed nation.

In October 2018, Penny, from North Carolina, was diagnosed with a tumor after an MRI scan, and doctors were talking about performing surgery. However, Penny chose to believe God's promise from First Peter 2:24 instead, and stand on it:

> *Who Himself bore our sins in His own body on the tree, that we, having died to sins, might live for righteousness—by whose stripes you were healed* (1 Peter 2:24).

In March 2019, Penny attended a healing conference where I spoke forth a word of knowledge that there was something behind the ear. Twice it was said that the Lord is healing it. Penny knew it was the tumor in her brain, and she had the assurance that she was healed. This prophetic word of knowledge was a confirmation of what Penny was already believing God for, and He brought forth the manifestation during the conference.

Now, Penny is completely off all medicines and no MRI scans are required for two years. She is now committed to telling people, especially in the cancer ward, about her healing and is praying for others who also need a healing touch from God.

This is how it should be—we receive healing and then we release healing. And those we minister to receive and then they release this same healing power of our Great Physician—Jesus—to those in their arena of influence. This spiritual multiplication equation of God's healing power continues to increase.

Whether we are sharing the Gospel of Jesus Christ with signs and wonders, confirming the message one-on-one with a neighbor or in a small group or before the masses, God designed us to make disciples by His example, revealed throughout the Gospels. And God desires that we, His followers, are healed in spirit, soul, and in our physical body. Jesus commands us to do the same as spoken of in the Great Commission found in Mark 16:15-18.

Healing is not geographical. It has nothing to do with where we are born, where we presently live, or how much money we do or don't have. It has to do with the power of the blood of Jesus Christ that redeems us from our sin and the consequences of those sins—death. And whether premature death comes in the form of sickness and disease or through tragedy—we have been redeemed from it. All we have to do is believe God for our miracle. And even if we don't presently believe this way, we can study the Word of God and learn how to believe.

Perhaps, as you begin to read this book, you may be so full of doubt and unbelief about the healing power of Jesus that you are reasoning away in your mind why you think this is not true, or perhaps to you it's just an oddity, or even isolated cases. If so, I challenge you to read on.

I also want to interject another thought for you to consider, *Just because you live in a developed nation, does this mean you must first try all human options before you turn to God for your healing? Or is it possible to jump into this supernatural tsunami wave of healing and receive your miracle from God?*

Okay, I've shared real-life healing testimonies from both developing and developed nations to prove to you that the healing power of the Lord is not geographical. I've imparted to you the prophetic vision the Lord gave to me about this tsunami wave of healing. And now to fully step into this glorious wave of healing, we should take a good look at what a tsunami is and the workings behind one, and compare a natural tsunami to this supernatural tsunami wave of healing glory that is upon us. This teaching is full of revelation. Are you ready?

What Is a Tsunami?

In the natural:

> Tsunamis are giant waves caused by earthquakes or volcanic eruptions under the sea. Out in the depths of the ocean, tsunami waves do not dramatically increase in height. But as the waves travel inland, they build up to higher and higher heights as the depth of the ocean decreases. The speed of

tsunami waves depends on ocean depth rather than the distance from the source of the wave. Tsunami waves may travel as fast as jet planes over deep waters, only slowing down when reaching shallow waters. While tsunamis are often referred to as tidal waves, this name is discouraged by oceanographers because tides have little to do with these giant waves.[2]

We read what a tsunami is in the natural realm, now let's delve into the spiritual sphere, where the supernatural realm of God quakes and erupts with much greater power. Spiritual waves of healing are formed out in the deep and travel inland and overtake the wickedness the spirits of fear and death cause in these latter days.

How a Tsunami Starts

In the earthly realm, according to our general study, one of the ways tsunamis are triggered is by a large earthquake near or under the ocean.

Spiritually speaking, this tsunami wave of healing glory begins the same way a natural tsunami does—with a great earthquake. This earthquake is recorded in Matthew 28:2 at the resurrection of Jesus when the angel of the Lord came and rolled the stone away and globally announced that Jesus Christ was no longer dead, but risen just as He had said. In this resurrection power of Christ we can and do have a tsunami wave of healing glory.

> *Now after the Sabbath, as the first day of the week began to dawn, Mary Magdalene and the other Mary came to see the tomb. And behold, there was a great earthquake; for an angel of the Lord descended from heaven, and came and rolled back the stone from the door, and sat on it. His countenance was like lightning, and his clothing as white as snow. And the guards shook for fear of him, and became like dead men* (Matthew 28:1-4).

Can you imagine the supernatural power that was released into the physical earth at this moment? I lived in Guatemala for twenty-five years on the Motagua Fault Zone and near a couple of active volcanoes, so by experience I, like everyone living in this part of the world, developed a healthy respect for the power that lies deep beneath the earth's surface. I know by the power of my five natural senses the various ways the earth shakes and rolls, and how the buildings move and sway, and have heard the groanings of the earth during and in between these frightfully powerful events. I have heard and felt the "Fuego (Fire) Volcano" rumble day and night until it spews out of its mouth deadly, liquid fire hundreds or thousands of feet, even miles into the air. And even witnessed its deadly aftermath that instantly buried countless numbers of people.

The earth is filled with power that can alter the events of life instantly, but even still, there is no tremor, earthquake, or volcanic explosion that can compare to that glorious day when the release of His resurrection power caused the earth to quake violently. That supernatural earthquake suddenly released our rescue from the vile darkness of hell and secured our eternity in Heaven with Jesus Christ Himself! Now that's supernatural power to honor and respect!

Tsunami Waves of Healing During Meetings

I have shared with you real-life experiences in the natural concerning the force within the earth, but now I will share with you the real-life supernatural power of God. For years I have been a witness to these waves during healing seminars and conferences. In the beginning of a Holy Spirit-led service, the musicians and the singers usher in the first wave that soothes the soul, the mind, and the emotions and leads people into the presence of God.

As I lay a firm biblical foundation, I see the Spirit shake the fallow (untilled or uncultivated) ground. And as this wave of the Word of God begins to build out in the deep realm of the Spirit, it reveals the carnality, doubt, and unbelief in the people. And the truth in the power of the blood begins to set the people free, as a wave of repentance washes in. And with each point in the message, a wave of expectancy flows into the hearts of the people in greater measure. Part of the greater measure that I witness in these waves is with the baptism of the Holy Spirit.

For the past seven to eight years, there has been a resurgence of this baptism. The altars are filled with people receiving their supernatural language. Even in denominations that have taught against this for many years, they want to be taught the things of the Spirit and pray in the power of tongues. I believe the reason for this resurgence is to empower God's people with His might for these last days. There comes a point of no return when, after being in the deep waters with Holy Spirit, His great healing power is released and moves speedily—and the tsunami wave of healing glory rushes over the people.

A real-life example of this is when I was ministering in Purcellville, Virginia, and we witnessed a tsunami wave of healing glory break forth with such power that it was undeniably evident that Holy Spirit was loosed in that place. I was ministering the healing power to many when suddenly, I touched the next person and the healing power rushed straight through that section of people. Their healings were suddenly and simultaneously manifesting with no effort. To their amazement and great pleasure, their backs, necks, shoulders, hips, knees, ankles, and arches were instantly renewed.

I have often heard during this point in the meetings the ushers call out, "Slow down, Becky!" But I can't, it's not me, it's the power of His might working through me. I have done everything possible to cooperate with Him, to build the right atmosphere where He is free to move at His will. And when we reach this level in the supernatural realm, He moves fast and furious over His people with a vengeance against the wicked power of the enemy.

One of these fast and furious waves is against the spirit of death that I taught in my previously published book, *Conquering the Spirit of Death*. Again, when Holy Spirit says to me, *"Call the people forward who are battling with cancer,"* the altars fill up with many people afflicted with this demon of death that is fueled by a spirit of fear. I sense great healing glory flow in and throughout these people. And the testimonies keep pouring in that many are supernaturally healed. Not only are people being healed from cancer in great numbers, but from whatever disease that has them bound to this spirit of death.

Waves Recap:

1. First, a wave of worship.
2. Then comes the wave of repentance.
3. Afterward, a wave of revelation truth found only in the Word of God.
4. In the midst of these incoming waves rushes in a wave of the baptism of Holy Spirit with the evidence of praying in tongues.
5. Then comes a fast and furious wave against the spirit of death.
6. Then a most powerful wave of healing glory that cannot be stopped.

Why am I spending time sharing with you what I have been witnessing during these meetings? Because they are examples of what is happening around the world, whether we are inside or outside, in a conference, or out on the street. Wherever God's people are, this tsunami wave of healing glory is breaking forth.

God wants to use you for His glory in these chaotic times to:

- Usher in His presence through true worship

- Lead people through repentance
- Lay a firm biblical foundation with a Word from Him
- Empower people around you with the baptism of the Holy Spirit
- Activate your God-given authority over the spirit of death
- Step into this supernatural tsunami wave of healing glory

This is how Jesus witnessed to the lost when He walked the earth, and this is the power He has given to you and me to gather in this great end times harvest with signs and wonders that no one can deny.

Do Not Be Afraid

Let's continue on with this glorious account:

> *But the angel answered and said to the women, "Do not be afraid, for I know that you seek Jesus who was crucified. He is not here; for He is risen, as He said. Come, see the place where the Lord lay. And go quickly and tell His disciples that He is risen from the dead, and indeed He is going before you into Galilee; there you will see Him. Behold, I have told you"* (Matthew 28:5-7).

It also says in Matthew 28:8 that not only did they go out quickly, but they went out with fear and great joy. This word *fear*, found in Strong's G5401, means "alarm or fright:—be afraid, + exceedingly, fear, terror." Just like the women in the tomb, we should have this same alarm sounding off within our spirit, the urgency of the times that we are living in. We should care more about the eternal well-being of the people who are not in right standing with Jesus than we do about ourselves who know we are eternally saved. Galatians 6:10 in the Amplified Version of the Bible says it like this:

So then, while we [as individual believers] have the opportunity, let us do good to all people [not only being helpful, but also doing that which promotes their spiritual well-being], and especially [be a blessing] to those of the household of faith (born-again believers).

A spirit of fear is the forerunner to a spirit of death. And we have been a witness of a recent pandemic—COVID-19—and how quickly it spread throughout the earth. What caused this pandemic to spread as fast as it did? Fear. It was fueled by a spirit of fear, but God clearly says, *"Do not be afraid."* As we look at this portion of Scripture we see what can happen when we say "No!" to fear, and "Yes!" to courage. Courage leads to resurrection power and life; it causes us to see our Lord, which then leads to joy. And joy is a supernatural power that heals and strengthens us. This courage and joy are the supernatural keys we need to overcome the spirits of fear and death.

Great Joy

As we study Matthew 28:8, we read about *"great joy."* Are our hearts filled with an overwhelming sense of great joy with the thought of His return? During the COVID-19 pandemic people felt fearful and isolated—just what the enemy wanted. Daily work and normal activity came to a standstill, and people became filled with anxiety and depression set it.

It's important that we talk about this now. Do you feel like your life is going nowhere? I challenge you to no longer allow the enemy to play with your mind. As a believer you are never just spinning your wheels going from no place to nowhere. You are Heaven bound, and your Creator is creating a special place for you in your forever home. Allow your imagination to ponder on this promise from Jesus, *"And if I go and prepare a place for you, I will come back again and I will take you to Myself, so that where I am you may be also"* (John 14:3 AMP).

Settle the matter in your heart once and for all that you are chosen by God and very special to Him. Let your mind linger in these words from Titus 2:13-14 from the Amplified Version of the Bible:

> *Awaiting and confidently expecting the [fulfillment of our] blessed hope and the glorious appearing of our great God and Savior, Christ Jesus, who [willingly] gave Himself [to be crucified] on our behalf to redeem us and purchase our freedom from all wickedness, and to purify for Himself a chosen and very special people to be His own possession, who are enthusiastic for doing what is good.*

Just think, in the next twinkling of an eye we may meet Him in the air and be eternally transformed from the physical to the spiritual realm.

> *Listen very carefully, I tell you a mystery [a secret truth decreed by God and previously hidden, but now revealed]; we will not all sleep [in death], but we will all be [completely] changed [wondrously transformed], in a moment, in the twinkling of an eye, at [the sound of] the last trumpet call. For a trumpet will sound, and the dead [who believed in Christ] will be raised imperishable, and we will be [completely] changed [wondrously transformed]* (1 Corinthians 15:51-52 AMP).

And it gives me great joy to envision these promises coming to pass in our lifetime. With absolute confidence I do believe in the return of the Lord. And the more I confess my belief in these promises, the bolder in my faith I become. I pray the following verse is true for you:

> *May the God of hope fill you with all joy and peace in believing [through the experience of your faith] that by the power of the*

Holy Spirit you will abound in hope and overflow with confidence in His promises (Romans 15:13 AMP).

Run Quickly

So they went out quickly from the tomb with fear and great joy, and ran to bring His disciples word (Matthew 28:8).

Matthew 28:8 says *"they went out quickly."* According to Strong's G5035, this word *quickly* means "speedily, without delay." Has the Lord been speaking to your heart to get moving and tell the people around you of His soon return? Have you been obedient? If not, why?

About three years ago, the Spirit of the Lord spoke to my heart and said to me, *"Run! Run as fast as you can. Run as hard as you are able. Take as many with you who will come. The time is shorter than you think. Run!"* This command resounds within my spirit, and I have been doing just as He says, *"Run!"* And I impart this same command of the Lord to you now, "Run!"

The Height of the Wave

Let's continue to build upon the teaching of this tsunami wave of healing glory so that you can ride it and release its power to those around you.

The National Ocean Service gives us important information about the height of tsunami waves: "Out in the depths of the ocean, tsunami waves do not dramatically increase in height. But as the waves travel inland, they build up to higher and higher heights as the depth of the ocean decreases."

Now let's shed revelation on this comparison of the natural height of the wave to the spiritual tsunami wave so we can release the supernatural power of it. Out in the depths of the ocean the height of the wave is not seen, but it is out in these depths that the tsunami is formed. And so too in the supernatural realm it is out in the deep depths of the workings of Holy Spirit this is formed and released. But as the wave travels inland where the people in need are, the height of this great tsunami wave of healing glory is seen, and its power is released. And the height of this wave is formed by the deep power of the love of God, which we will talk more in-depth about in Chapter 8, "The Healing Power of God's Love."

Warning Signs of a Tsunami

From the SMS Tsunami Warning webpage there are the following warning signs of an approaching tsunami that helps us understand the signs of a natural tsunami before discussing the supernatural tsunami wave of healing glory.

SMS website informs its readers with the following warning:

> Fortunately, a few natural warning signs can help you understand that a tsunami is approaching and they can be easily recognized. They include:
>
> - Strong ground shaking from an earthquake: if you are on the coast and there is an earthquake, it may have caused a tsunami, so escape immediately to higher ground or inland, avoiding river valleys;
> - Unusual sea-level fluctuations: a noticeable rapid rise or fall in coastal waters is a sign that there may be a tsunami approaching. If you see the water recede quickly and unexpectedly from a beach exposing the ocean floor (the so-called drawback) or a sudden rise of the sea level, escape immediately to higher ground or inland, avoiding river valleys;
> - Abnormally huge wave: the first wave in a tsunami wave train is usually not the largest, so if you see an abnormally huge wave, even bigger waves could be coming soon. Run

immediately to higher ground or inland, avoiding river valleys;

- Loud ocean roar: if you hear a roaring sound offshore, similar to that of a train or jet aircraft, a tsunami may be approaching, so escape immediately to higher ground or inland, avoiding river valleys.[3]

Spiritually speaking the earth is quaking, and supernatural alarms are sounding for us to head to higher ground. We will discuss this further in Chapter 4, "How to Escape to Higher Ground."

The Drawback

We have also witnessed a spiritual drawback over the past several years that has exposed, brought to light, the ocean floor of our spiritual condition—and quite often we have not liked what has been exposed. To continue on in the spiritual context, in very recent times the shores of this land have even appeared to be waterless, dry, and to many it felt more like a desert with little activity than an active seashore.

But just as a tsunami behaves in the natural, so too in the supernatural realm a mighty surge of power has been building out in the deep seas, and now it's hitting the shores and working its way inland toward the center of our hearts. Anyone willing to be immersed in its healing power can receive their long-awaited miracle, and many are doing this very thing—immersing themselves and being healed.

Now I'm at another healing service, this one is in North Carolina. The musicians and the singers are leading the way, when Holy Spirit tells me to go and anoint a particular singer with oil. I go and do so straightaway. Well, this woman, Margaret is slain in the Spirit, and begins to weep as she senses an intense burning heat, like a well-stoked fire below her feet, but at the same time she can see it raining over all the people.

At the same time, I speak out prophetically over the people and Holy Spirit is drawing back and revealing the hidden sins among the group. A mighty cleansing began of repentance—from sin to deliverance, from demon spirits to physical healing broke forth; and in that order, conviction, repentance, salvation, baptism of Holy Spirit, deliverance, and then physical healing manifested.

We've read and even reminded ourselves that vengeance belongs to the Lord (Romans 12:19 NKJV). And indeed it does. But what I am witnessing in this tsunami wave of healing glory is that the destructive power in it, isn't against us—it's against satan and all of his wicked works rising up against us. And the power pushing this wave inland is the pure and perfect love of God.

> *Do not repay anyone evil for evil. Be careful to do what is right in the eyes of everyone. If it is possible, as far as it depends on you, live at peace with everyone. Do not take revenge, my dear friends, but leave room for God's wrath, for it is written: "It is mine to avenge; I will repay," says the Lord* (Romans 12:17-19 NIV).

An Even Bigger Wave Is on the Way

The information from the SMS website explains that "the first wave in a tsunami wave train is usually not the largest, so if you see an abnormally huge wave, even bigger waves could be coming soon."

This supernatural tsunami wave of healing glory continues to increase in size and power. More of His healing glory is being released with each wave of this train. And it is transforming the lives of an even greater sum of people.

I am witnessing a great increase at the altar of the Lord where God's people are publicly confessing their sins. There is a hunger for the uncompromised Word of the Lord, a saturation of His holy presence that sets the captives free. The altars are filled with God's people being filled with the baptism of the Holy Spirit praying unashamedly in tongues. And His miraculous power is busting loose everywhere.

Even during the shutdown of everyday life with the Coronavirus pandemic and the orders to social distance from one another and not hold public meetings, the healing power of Holy Spirit has not stopped. People continue to believe and receive the manifestation of their much needed miracles. The following is a beautiful testimony of this bigger wave to empower your faith.

On February 21, 2020, at 1:27 a.m. I receive the following prayer request from a woman named Diana:

> "Dear Becky, I thank you and God for your ability to help people through prayer. My cousin has been diagnosed with a rare disease called Amyotrophic Lateral Sclerosis (ALS). It's a fast progressing illness and now he is tied to bed, it's very difficult for him to walk and even speak. He is dependent on other people to help him daily with everything. I am asking for a miracle in Jesus' name for this illness to disappear from his body. Amen."

> On March 3, 2020, at 3:13 p.m. I find her email among many other requests for healing prayer. I read and respond with faith:

> "Diana, in the name of Jesus, I renounce this ALS, and the spirit of death that goes with it. I declare that his nervous system is recreated and that weakened muscles are strengthened and made whole and all physical functions are restored for the glory of the Lord, amen."

> Then on May 4, 2020, at 5:14 a.m. I receive a response from Diana. She writes to testify with the following report:

"Dear Becky, it's a testimony. I praise God and you for miraculous healing for my cousin who was diagnosed from the incurable disease called ALS (Amyotrophic Lateral Sclerosis). Today I found out he is healed and no symptoms of the disease. I just want to thank you from my heart for your prayer back in March. God bless you. Praise God!"

And on May 7, 2020, at 2:18 p.m. in the midst of a long list of emails I find and read Diana's praise report and respond:

"Dear Diana, this is such wonderful news for your cousin and such a beautiful witness for many others who are inflicted with this disease, ALS. Praise the Lord for His goodness!! Amen! "

What a glorious testimony this is! And you realize that I never met her cousin. I never spoke with him personally. I didn't lay healing hands upon him. What I did do was not allow physical distance to become an issue in his healing process. I did not allow human reasoning or fear of this dreaded disease to detour my faith for his healing. And I honestly joined my faith with Diana's faith, prayed a sincere prayer of faith, trusted in God's healing promises, and allowed the healing to manifest.

Can you takes these steps of faith for the welfare of another person? Sure you can. The real question is are you willing to take the time to pray in faith for someone else in need. I believe you will.

Loud Roar

The final warning speaks of a loud ocean roar. The warnings are being sounded throughout the world via the Holy Scriptures and the voices of modern-day prophets.

And for those who fear these times, I add another thought for you to ponder; even though it is called the "end times," in essence it's an end to satan and his corruption—and a brand-new beginning, like turning the page in an exciting book for believers in our Messiah.

Let's get back to Matthew 28 for just a little while longer. I love the clash between the emotions of fear and joy, and how the supernatural power of joy overpowered Mary Magdalene and the other Mary as they ran in faith to see the tomb. There, the angel of the Lord proclaimed the good news about Jesus, *"Do not be afraid, for I know that you seek Jesus who was crucified. He is not here; for He is risen, as He said...."* (See Matthew 28:1-8.) They could only respond the way they did to this roaring message of faith because they truly believed. My prayer of faith for you, dear reader, is that you will hear the good news proclamation throughout this work, overcome the fear of these troubling times, and run in the supernatural power of joy. You too can raise the dead, heal the sick, open blind eyes, and set the captives free.

Spend time today and allow your thoughts to mull over the alarm that is sounding off in the supernatural realm during these days. Along with this supernatural alarm, allow this great joy to flood your soul. An encouraging thought to add to this moment of meditation from God's Word is found in Psalm 119:32 (NIV): *"I run in the path of your commands, for you have broadened my understanding."*

Prayer

Father God, as I allow my thoughts to mull over the spiritual alarms that are sounding off around us in these last days, I will not fear; instead, I choose to put on joy today accepting the fact that this is all an end to satan and his corruption. But for someone like me, who truly does believe in the saving grace of Your Son, my Savior Yeshua, this is all the beginning of something much greater than even my mind can imagine. I am called to immerse myself entirely into this supernatural tsunami wave of healing and illustrate with my life Your glory, not only in my body, but for those whom You have entrusted in my care, and to all people everywhere. May I wholeheartedly embrace Your resurrection power and release this great healing power everywhere I go. In the name of Yeshua, I pray, amen.

As we broaden our spiritual understanding of this supernatural tsunami wave of healing glory it's time to soak ourselves in the first supernatural wave of worship, and learn what God really intends for us to do with this life expression.

Faith Assignment

For the next thirty days, I am assigning you to voice-activate your faith with praise for fifteen minutes each day to thank the Lord for this supernatural tsunami wave of healing glory that you are called to be part of. Start by worshipping the Lord for His greatness and for the healing power He released for us by the power of His blood. Start by confessing the following confession of praise and then add your own words from your heart:

"Holy, holy, holy is the Lord of hosts; the whole earth is full of Your glory!" (see Isaiah 6:3). Jehovah Rapha—the God who heals, I worship You and the power of Your redeeming blood to heal us in spirit, soul, and body. I thank You that You choose to bear my griefs, all sickness and disease that attacks me and my loved ones. I give glory to Your most holy name for carrying my sorrows, my physical and mental pain. You were plagued and slaughtered, wounded and defiled because of my transgression, my rebellion against my God. You were bruised and crushed for my iniquities, my perversity, and for my sin. You were chastised for my peace, my welfare, my health and prosperity. And by Your stripes, Your healing whips, I am healed and made whole (Isaiah

53:4-5). I worship You, Jehovah Rapha. You are the God who heals (Exodus 15:26). In Jesus' name, I pray, amen.

This confession of praise is inspired from the Holy Scriptures. Use it to start your praise moment and then be creative and personal with words of worship from your heart and thank Him for divine opportunities to come to you to minister to others.

Questions to Ponder and Answer for Chapter 1: Tsunami Wave of Healing Glory

1. Spiritually speaking, how did this tsunami wave of healing glory begin?

_____

_____

_____

_____

2. Where is this wave recorded?

_____

_____

_____

_____

3. Recap; write out the six spiritual waves you read about in this chapter.

_____

_____

_____

_____

4. Why did I share with you what I have been witnessing during these meetings?

_____

_____

_____

5. What does God want to do with you during these chaotic times?

_____

_____

_____

6. What alarm should have sounded off within your spirit at this time?

_____

_____

_____

7. During these times, what should you care more about?

_____

_____

_____

Personal Assessment

What do I need from the Lord? Do I back away from His healing power? Have I been in doubt and unbelief concerning His mighty power to heal? Why do I doubt this move of Holy Spirit to heal us? Or do I believe He wills to heal others, but not me? Why do I believe like this? Do I want to be part of this mighty end times move of the Spirit to heal people in spirit, soul (the mind and the emotions), and in the physical body too? Do I care about people around me who are eternally lost?

Group Discussion

Together as a group, discuss steps you can take to believe and activate your faith to be part of this supernatural tsunami wave of healing glory. Talk about how you have seen this supernatural drawback that has exposed the ocean floor of your spiritual condition. Speak from your heart about having to overcome fear of the current troubling events. Break into smaller groups and pray for encouragement and joy to return to your spiritual hearts.

Notes

1. Becky Dvorak, *Greater Than Magic* (Shippensburg, PA: Destiny Image Publishers, 2014), 164.
2. "What is a tsunami?" NOAA; https://oceanservice.noaa.gov/facts/tsunami.html, accessed October 15, 2019.
3. "Tsunami: warning signs"; SMS TSUNAMI WARNING; https://www.sms-tsunami-warning.com/pages/tsunami-warning -signs#.XaYT2Z7nIU; accessed October 15, 2019.

A Life-Expression of Worship

Word of the Lord

The Spirit of the Lord would say to you this day,

> Prepare your hearts for the spiritual battles that are rising up against you. Enter into My gates with praise. Worship Me in spirit and in truth. Raise up the standard of the blood of the Lamb against that unfriendly foe. Take him down with the power of worship. Build the atmosphere for the power of My Spirit to inhabit. I inhabit the praises of My people. Freely share with one another in psalms, hymns, and spiritual songs. Offer up to Me a life-expression of worship, and you will overcome in these days of tribulation.

The Spirit of God is releasing waves filled with supernatural healing power that are encompassing the earth for His glory. The first healing wave we are diving into is worship.

Worship is such an important part of our relationship with our Lord, and yet it can be so misunderstood by the Body of Christ. Because it is one of the major waves flooding the earth in these latter days, we cannot afford confusion or dissension among ourselves. Worship is a powerful tool to be wielded with skill and determination. We must cut the enemy's cord of discord, plug into the power source of the Spirit, and learn to worship in spirit and in truth.

There are many ways to worship and different ways to play upon the strings of our hearts. We can worship with our words of faith, and worship with instruments with or without singing. We can vocalize our praise in our earthly languages or in our heavenly tongues. There are times when we worship with the volume turned down low as a whisper, and other times with strong shouts of praise. With reverent attitudes we raise our hands to worship the Lord, or on our knees with our heads bowed low—and at times we are prostrate and sprawled out across the floor.

During raging spiritual battles, we march with a militant attitude against the attack of the enemy. And other times we blow the shofar; and with timbrel in hand, we dance for jubilee. Our lives truly are expressions of worship to our Most High God.

The Father Is Seeking True Worshippers

The Father is seeking those who will worship Him in spirit and in truth. You might be wondering what it means to worship in spirit and in truth. God is Spirit; and when we become born-again, we become an eternal-spirit being bound for eternity with Him. But while on this earth He wants people who will worship Him in spirit, not the flesh.

And may I be perfectly clear here, this is not about the style of music you use during a gathering of believers. Quite frankly, you can sing the best-loved hymns and not unite with His Spirit. You can also have the most popular Christian artist sing his or her heart out and completely bypass the Spirit. You can even be somewhere in between the two and still compromise Holy Spirit. So, it is not about the type of music you wish to use during your times of community worship. And it's important to add that worship is not limited to singing and playing instruments, there are other ways to express our worship.

We have established that worship is more than singing praises to God, but there may remain a bit of confusion. Just what is worship? Worship is something we do that stems from a heart attitude that God has great value to us. And when we carry His value within our hearts and then enter into His habitat—where He is—we touch His heart with our hearts. And the only way to do this is to worship the One True God. Even if we are in the midst of a corporate time of worship with others, as true worshippers, we forsake all others around us and purposefully aim to minister to God alone.

Our Lord is yearning for us to enter into His domain—His presence. We do this by tapping into His heart, worshipping Him for who He is, honoring His deity, and acknowledging His greatness.

You may also be wondering what it means to worship Him in truth. It means having the revelation knowledge about who God is. When you know who He is, you believe in Him. You believe He is who He says He is, and has done exactly as He tells us in His Word—the Holy Bible. The only way to remain in the presence of the Spirit of Truth is to make a lifestyle out of the study of the Word of God. Continuously reading, studying, declaring, and living what His words tell us to do. The more we read and study the Word, the greater the revelation of who He is, and out of this truth comes the freedom and desire to worship Him—the Spirit of Truth.

> *But a time is coming and is already here when the true worshipers will worship the Father in spirit [from the heart, the inner self] and in truth; for the Father seeks such people to be His worshipers* (John 4:23 AMP).

Worship Is a Matter of the Heart

Worship is indeed a matter of the heart. It is a reflection of what is stored up in the heart for our Lord. As I meditate upon the act of worship, I am reminded of the woman from Luke 7:36-50 who knows all too well that she is a sinner, but recognizes the Grace Giver—Jesus—to forgive her of her sins. And with a true heart of worship gives the best she has, a costly alabaster box of fragranced oil and begins to minister to Jesus by washing His feet with her tears filled with personal pain. And yes, as we read her testimony we see that a religious spirit rises up against her act of worship and devalues her gift to the Messiah, trying to shame her at the feet of her Lord.

But the grace of God has always and always will give His unmerited favor to the one who worships Him in spirit and in truth. This woman, despite her past that disqualifies her as one deserving of grace, overcomes the scorn of the religious community and the oppressing powers of guilt and shame. In doing so, she humbly positions herself at the feet of the One with the authority to forgive her and enters into the realm of the few who actually worship Messiah in spirit and in truth.

Principles of Worship

The woman's actions involve the following principles of worship:

- Acknowledgment of who Yeshua is—the Grace Giver and Forgiver.
- Recognition of God's greatness by humbling herself at His feet.
- Giving the best she has—a costly alabaster box of fragranced oil.
- The personal gift of herself—her brokenness by shedding her tears.
- Ministering to the personal needs of Jesus—washing His feet.
- Defying the accuser.

Celebration Worship

In Exodus 15:1-21 we read the jubilant songs of praise to God for the miraculous ways He rescued Moses and the Israelites from Pharaoh and his army. In the first nineteen verses we read the triumphant song of Moses and the sons of Israel. And in verses 20 and 21, we read of prophetess Miriam's joyful response and how she and the daughters of Israel with timbrel in hand set their feet to dancing and their mouths to singing songs of praise and worship for all the Lord God Jehovah had done for them.

This type of worship is loud, spontaneous, joyful, and filled with acts of lively worship such as dance, hand clapping, waving flags, jumping, marching, etc. This type of worship is described in Strong's H1984 as *hâlal.* A primitive root; to be clear (originally of sound, but usually of color); to shine; hence to make a show; to boast; and thus to be (clamorously) foolish; to rave; causatively to celebrate; also to stultify.[1]

Psalm 100:1-5 encourages us to:

> *Make a joyful shout to the Lord, all you lands! Serve the Lord with gladness; come before His presence with singing. Know that the Lord, He is God; it is He who has made us, and not we ourselves; we are His people and the sheep of His pasture. Enter into His gates with thanksgiving, and into His courts with praise. Be thankful to Him, and bless His name. For the Lord is good; His mercy is everlasting, and His truth endures to all generations.*

I realize that times are tough for many, but we need to activate the supernatural power of the joy of the Lord in our lives again. This celebration worship is just what the Great Physician, our Lord Himself, would have us do to heal and break off the spirit of heaviness. It's uplifting to sing of the good reports of all that the Lord has done and continues to do for us. These tunes of celebration worship seem to stick around in our mind and emotions—as if clinging to a refreshing word.

Actions of Worship

Actions of worship involve the following principles:

- Corporate worship
- Lively songs, rhythm instruments, and dancing
- Joyful and loud

Together they proclaim the marvelous acts of God and acknowledge Him as Deliverer.

Warfare Worship

Body of Christ, we are facing real fiery times. The heat of the world's spiritual furnace is heating up against us. Our enemy, satan, knows full well that his time is short. And his main goal is to steal, kill, and destroy us in any way he can with the limited time he has left. With this being said, we need to be aware that his attacks against us will be sudden, strong, and wicked. His desire is that we recant our faith and turn our backs on our Lord and Savior. He and his demonic force are stoking the furnace in their efforts to stop and defeat us. How do we overcome this great evil in these last days? We fan the flame of devotion and honor, and worship the Lord's most holy name.

Shadrach, Meshach, and Abed-Nego faced the same fiery trial— bow to the idol or face death (see Daniel 3). They were given the opportunity to recant their faith, but they boldly held their ground, even though this meant death by fire for choosing not to deny God, the Father. And even though they obeyed God, we should make note that they still had to face the consequences of their defiance to the evil-driven Nebuchadnezzar and enter into that fiery furnace.

But they had settled in their hearts to remain faithful to the One True God and face pain, suffering, and even death. Taking a stand against the evil of this world is to enter into spiritual warfare. God could have rearranged events and spared them from this suffering, but He did not. What He did instead was allow them to operate in the realm of extreme warfare worship and put their lives on the line for their love for God.

What I am building up to say is that yes, we are facing real fiery times now as believers—and at the same time, God is using our lives as a witness of worship to Him to the world. Will we activate our faith through these burning hot times and allow ourselves to pass through whatever the consequence may be to worship our Lord? And how do we submit ourselves to such possible consequences? We submit by:

- Pledging our allegiance to God
- Taking a stand of faith against evil
- Refusing to give in to the spirit of fear
- Trusting God with our lives
- Declaring words of faith
- Acting on our words of faith

A real-life possibility for us in these turbulent times could be that we have to take the "mark of the beast" or face negative consequences and be denied basic necessities such as food, shelter, work opportunities, health insurance, and medical attention. We could even face death.

Revelation 14:9-11 warns us about the eternal consequences if we receive the mark of the beast:

> *...If anyone worships the beast and his image, and receives his mark on his forehead or on his hand, he himself shall also drink of the wine of the wrath of God, which is poured out full strength into the cup of His indignation. He shall be tormented*

with fire and brimstone in the presence of the holy angels and in the presence of the Lamb. And the smoke of their torment ascends forever and ever; and they have no rest day or night, who worship the beast and his image, and whoever receives the mark of his name.

Being familiar with the Scriptures, we know we have to take a stand against evil and refuse to deny God. We can only do this by pledging our allegiance to God first—being completely sold out for Jesus. This means putting our trust completely in the hands of God—even with our very lives and well-being. We cannot give in to a spirit of fear; rather we must declare words of faith and act upon them.

Shadrach, Meshach, and Abed-Nego did this very thing. Their famous words of faith to King Nebuchadnezzar are recorded in Daniel 3:17-18:

*If that is the case, **our God whom we serve is able to deliver us** from the burning fiery furnace, and He will deliver us from your hand, O king. But if not, let it be known to you, O king, that **we do not serve your gods, nor will we worship the gold image which you have set up**.*

The only way these three men or any one of us could step up to the plate of faith and declare such dedication to our God is if we first activate the power of worship that is true and of the Spirit. God is requiring each of us to lay our faith on the line through these times of trials and persecution and allow our lives to be an expression of worship for Him and for others to witness our testimony.

These men of God did just that—and supernaturally they did not die, their clothing did not even smell of smoke. Others saw that Jesus was with them in that blazing fiery furnace; and as a result, the heart of King Nebuchadnezzar was won over to God.

Now I, Nebuchadnezzar, praise and extol and honor the King of heaven, all of whose works are truth, and His ways justice. And those who walk in pride He is able to put down (Daniel 4:37).

The fiery furnace we face may not be an actual furnace, it may be a disease raging against us, or family relationships, or a myriad of other issues. But whatever it may be, no matter the intensity of the blazing flames of the ungodly furnace we face, true worship will give us the grace and strength we need to enter into warfare worship and overcome.

The following are three Scripture verses about living life with worship to strengthen your faith:

- I will sing to the Lord as long as I live; I will sing praise to my God while I have my being (Psalm 104:33).

- Let everything that has breath praise the Lord. Praise the Lord! (Psalm 150:6).

- Because Your lovingkindness is better than life, my lips shall praise You. Thus I will bless You while I live; I will lift up my hands in Your name (Psalm 63:3-4).

We Are Kings and Priests unto God

Do you realize that if you are a born-again Christian, you are a priest? The Bible says in First Peter 2:9 that we are a royal priesthood. But let's face it, most of us are uncomfortable with the title "priest." In fact, when we hear the term priest, what comes to our minds is a picture of a man wearing a special collar or robe sprinkling people with holy water. Right? That makes us feel uncomfortable with who God called us to be—a priest unto Himself.

But perhaps, if we remove the religiosity from the term priest and learn what our duties as a priest unto God are, we will be more comfortable with this calling from God, our Father. What is a priest? A priest is someone who approaches God on behalf of others. A priest is an intercessor. And whenever we pray for others, we are fulfilling our priestly duty.

> But you are a chosen generation, a **royal priesthood**, a holy nation, His own special people, that you may proclaim the praises of Him who called you out of darkness into His marvelous light (1 Peter 2:9).

Not only are we called by God unto His priesthood, but to a royal priesthood. In other words, we are of royal blood—the atoning blood of the Messiah. Knowing that the confirmation of two or three witnesses is very important to establish a truth, let's gaze upon a second witness from Revelation 1:5-6 and discuss what it has to say about this matter:

> And from Jesus Christ, the faithful witness, the firstborn from the dead, and the ruler over the kings of the earth. To Him who loved us and washed us from our sins in His own blood, and has made us **kings and priests** to His God and Father, to Him be glory and dominion forever and ever. Amen.

Did you catch that? Yeshua, also made us "kings" to His God, the Father as well.

Kings are of royal blood, they are given authority to rule and reign. We as believers live so far below what God has created us for. We are given authority to rule and reign over satan and all of his wicked works (see Luke 10:19), and with this same authority we are to subdue the earth, and have dominion over it (see Genesis 1:26-29).

As priests and kings unto God, what do we do with this calling?

Build Your Sanctuary for God

We should have a quiet place with God. A place we go to get away from the noise and the distractions in life. I know of families that have actually built a chapel onto the side of their house, equipped with an altar and all. But most of us can't do this, nor do we need to. The sanctuary I'm speaking of is not built with human hands, but with the heart.

I've had several different settings for my personal sanctuary with God. When we lived in Guatemala, my sanctuary was on the flat rooftop of the house under the stars when everyone else was safely tucked in bed. And I have to admit, I miss this spiritual place.

My first night in fulfilling the priestly calling, while praying in my heavenly tongues, I dedicated the rooftop as my sanctuary, my special place to God. I spread anointing oil over that place. I walked that rooftop under the stars and interceded as Holy Spirit directed. While doing so, I saw the first of many supernatural events that would take place on that rooftop.

That night while walking around my newly dedicated sanctuary, I saw a big ball of fire appear in front of me. I will be honest; at first, it unnerved me. Whether I turned to the right or to the left it followed me. I actually tried to step back and away from it, but there was nowhere to go. It then moved to the very center of the rooftop in direct alignment to where I was standing and it hovered for a slight moment, then it came with great speed right at me and upon me. And from that time forward, there was an increase in anointing; even people attending healing events see the angels traveling with me. They even see balls of fire leading them to the meeting place.

Very few people have ever been invited to come to my personal sanctuary and pray with me under the starlit sky. And those who were, witnessed what became common to me—angelic activity of a unique nature. While I would be walking and interceding under the guidance of Holy Spirit, when I would finish praying through an issue, I would see not falling stars, but ascending stars. I knew that I had prayed through the issue to its completion.

My ministry assistant, Palma, came to stay with us for a month in Guatemala. She was up on the rooftop with me, and to her delight she was amazed to see the very distinct ascending stars as we prayed through issues in life.

When I entered into warfare intercession, I sometimes saw fireballs come to the rescue with great force, landing on the ground of the children's home where we lived.

Now that I live in a populated area, the starlit sky is not as obvious, and I don't have a flat rooftop, so I have had to create another sanctuary. It's not so much about where you build your sanctuary, but when you enter it. Part of my current sanctuary is when I walk early in the morning for about one and a half to two hours, praying in the Spirit and in my earthly language. I praise the Lord. I declare His promises over me, my family, and the ministry. And I tell you, because of this lifestyle of worship in times of worshipful prayer—I am blessed.

You may be curious and wonder if I still have supernatural activity in my life—absolutely! I carry my sanctuary with God in my heart everywhere I go.

Almost every morning my ministry assistant walks over to our home and we pray in my office in the Spirit together as Holy Spirit leads us into the prophetic realm. My office is filled with supernatural activity too. He usually has us intercede not only for the ministry and our families, but also for the political arena and for end time events happening all around the world, and for our local pastor. In this sanctuary built with the heart, Holy Spirit takes us on spiritual journeys wherever He wills us to be to intercede with precision.

This is my quiet place, my sanctuary with God that I have built with my heart, not with my hands. I encourage you to do the same.

Rejoice always, pray without ceasing, in everything give thanks; for this is the will of God in Christ Jesus for you (1 Thessalonians 5:16-18).

Sharing in Corporate Worship

And let the peace of God rule in your hearts, to which also you were called in one body; and be thankful. Let the word of Christ dwell in you richly in all wisdom, teaching and admonishing one another in psalms and hymns and spiritual songs, singing with grace in your hearts to the Lord. And whatever you do in word or deed, do all in the name of the Lord Jesus, giving thanks to God the Father through Him (Colossians 3:15-17).

When following these scriptural guidelines, sharing in corporate worship when led by the Spirit is an amazing atmosphere for Holy Spirit to flow in and throughout the congregation. The benefits during this time are endless and not limited to human knowledge. When sharing in corporate worship like this, people are built up by the message of the Word, ministered to in the realm of the prophetic, are uplifted from the heaviness of the world, and healed and made whole in spirt, soul (mind and emotions), and in their physical bodies.

What is the difference between psalms and hymns and spiritual songs? Let's begin with psalms, which come from the Book of Psalms filled with verses of praise that were written by men under the inspiration of Holy Spirit to encourage our hearts during difficult times in life. A hymn is a song that we sing to praise, honor, and show our thankfulness to our Lord. Spiritual songs are not necessarily filled with praise and worship, but are founded upon the Scriptures and carry spiritual themes.

We should not fear submitting ourselves in sharing our corporate worship to the Lord in this manner, especially pastors. With your teaching and a little guidance, God's people will learn to follow the lead of Holy Spirit and enter into His presence with a fresh move of the Spirit that no one could have directed but God Himself. This will enrich and engage the people when you gather together. Free yourself to enter into this powerful realm of worship.

Corporate Worship

Corporate actions involve the following principles of worship:

- Corporate unity
- Spiritual sensitivity to Holy Spirit
- Act of faith to share in psalms and hymns and spiritual songs, and singing with grace
- Giving of thanks to our Lord

Giving—an Act of Worship

Giving is a form of worship and reveals what we treasure. We read in Matthew 6:21, *"For where your treasure is, there your heart will be also."* God loves a cheerful giver, which is explained to us in Second Corinthians 9:6-7 (NIV), *"Remember this: Whoever sows sparingly will also reap sparingly, and whoever sows generously will also reap generously. Each of you should give what you have decided in your heart to give, not reluctantly or under compulsion, for* **God loves a cheerful giver."**

To be a cheerful giver unto the Lord, we have to first *love God* and *value what He values*; and even more so, is the need to recognize *all we have comes from the Lord.* When we have these three points in order, we can be that cheerful giver who sows bountifully, generously. Our giving becomes well-pleasing to the Lord as an acceptable offering, a form of worship to Him.

In the realm of giving, we need to remember that we are to give tithes—a tenth of what we take in—to the place that feeds us spiritually. We receive our instructions for this in Malachi 3:10:

> *"Bring all the tithes into the storehouse, that there may be food in My house, and try Me now in this," says the Lord of hosts, "If I will not open for you the windows of heaven and pour out for*

you such blessing that there will not be room enough to receive it."

This tenth does not belong to us, it belongs to God. We are to give it to our local church so that the Word of God can be preached in our own neighborhoods. God wants us to offer this financial support with a joyful heart.

Offerings is anything above the tithe that we give. One area that is on God's list of priorities in this life is found in James 1:27: *"Pure and undefiled religion before God and the Father is this: to visit orphans and widows in their trouble, and to keep oneself unspotted from the world."* The care of orphans and widows is of extreme importance to God, our Father. And when we give to help them, we give directly to the Lord.

Then the King will say to those on His right hand, "Come, you blessed of My Father, inherit the kingdom prepared for you from the foundation of the world: for I was hungry and you gave Me food; I was thirsty and you gave Me drink; I was a stranger and you took Me in; I was naked and you clothed Me; I was sick and you visited Me; I was in prison and you came to Me."

Then the righteous will answer Him, saying, "Lord, when did we see You hungry and feed You, or thirsty and give You drink? When did we see You a stranger and take You in, or naked and clothe You? Or when did we see You sick, or in prison, and come to You?" And the King will answer and say to them, "Assuredly, I say to you, inasmuch as you did it to one of the least of these My brethren, you did it to Me." (Matthew 25:34-40).

There are many ways to give to advance the Kingdom of God, but we need to make sure our giving is actually honoring and worshipping Him, especially in these last days. We should only give offerings to ministries that are truly Christian based, where the full Gospel message of Jesus Christ is welcomed, endorsed, and shared.

Remember, giving is an act of worship and reveals what we treasure most.

Giving

Our actions of giving involve the following principles of worship:

- Honoring God with our tithes.
- Giving with joy unto the Lord.
- Worshiping God with our offerings.
- Supporting widows and the orphans.
- Using wisdom and giving only to ministries and organizations that are truly Christian.

The Power of Worship

God has given to us many spiritual weapons to fight our enemy; one of these weapons is the power of worship. Unadulterated worship is filled with supernatural power. We must not forget this in the days ahead of us. Regardless of what we the Church must face, let us hold on tight to this strategy for victory found in Revelation 12:11 (NIV): *"They triumphed over him by the blood of the Lamb and by the word of their testimony; they did not love their lives so much as to shrink from death."*

There are shining examples of victory throughout the Word of God to encourage our faith—let's review a few.

The Walls of Jericho Fall Down

In the Book of Joshua, chapter 6, we read the amazing testimony of how the walls of Jericho actually fall down. God gives a clear battle plan that is a bit out of the ordinary, and it involves the power of worship.

God instructs Joshua to have his army march around the city once a day for six days in a row. While marching, the soldiers sound their trumpets as the priests carry the Ark of the Covenant around the city of Jericho.

On the seventh day, the Israelites marched around the walls of Jericho seven times. And then at Joshua's command, the men release a powerful shout, and Jericho's walls miraculously fall down. The army races in and conquers the city.

I believe this is recorded not just for the sake of history, but to show us how we are to fight and overtake our enemy by the supernatural power of worship.

Delivered from Chains

Another amazing real-life story that involves the power of worship is from the New Testament in the Book of Acts, chapter 16. Again, this is not recorded just for history's sake, but for us to learn from Paul and Silas' example of faith and how to use the power of worship to free us from very difficult circumstances.

Paul and Silas suffer great pain and persecution after Paul casts a demon out of a slave girl. Her disgruntled masters were angry because they made their living using this possessed girl, so they dragged these two men of God to the marketplace and charged them before the authorities for sharing the Gospel and practicing what they preach. Paul and Silas were whipped and beaten, put in chains, and imprisoned.

But instead of wallowing in their pain, Paul and Silas began to pray, sing, and worship their God, which caused a supernatural transformation in the atmosphere and caused the earth to quake, open all the prison doors, and broke not only their chains but other prisoners' chains as well.

The guard woke up in a panic and was about to take his own life for fear that the prisoners escaped. But Paul and Silas called out to him, assured him that they were all there, and led him to the Lord. This newly saved guard took them to his home, fed them, tended to their wounds, and they walked away free to continue with the work of the Lord.

Dear church friend, we need to remember that worship is a powerful weapon that releases supernatural intervention during troubling and unbearable situations. It's time to worship in spirit and in truth as we move into the most amazing time in our history. And though we may pass through great trials and persecutions, we are equipped with the power of worship that will cause us to pass from one victory to another victory.

A Constant State of Worship

Imagine, if you will, with your spiritual eyes this scene from Heaven described in Revelation 4:2-11:

> *Immediately I was in the Spirit; and behold, a throne set in heaven, and One sat on the throne. And He who sat there was like a jasper and a sardius stone in appearance; and there was a rainbow around the throne, in appearance like an emerald. Around the throne were twenty-four thrones, and on the thrones I saw twenty-four elders sitting, clothed in white robes; and they had crowns of gold on their heads. And from the throne proceeded lightnings, thunderings, and voices. Seven lamps of fire were burning before the throne, which are the seven Spirits of God.*
>
> *Before the throne there was a sea of glass, like crystal. And in the midst of the throne, and around the throne, were four living creatures full of eyes in front and in back. The first living creature was like a lion, the second living creature like a calf, the third living creature had a face like a man, and the fourth living creature was like a flying eagle. The four living creatures, each having six wings, were full of eyes around and within.*

And they do not rest day or night, saying: "Holy, holy, holy, Lord God Almighty, who was and is and is to come!"

Whenever the living creatures give glory and honor and thanks to Him who sits on the throne, who lives forever and ever, the twenty-four elders fall down before Him who sits on the throne and worship Him who lives forever and ever, and cast their crowns before the throne, saying:

"You are worthy, O Lord, to receive glory and honor and power; for You created all things, and by Your will they exist and were created."

I have always been fascinated with the constant state of worship around the throne of God. Because it is going on in Heaven with such fervor, then it must be extremely important for us to know and to do on earth as well. As I write this, I hear these words in my spirit from the Lord's Prayer found in Matthew 6:9-13, *"Our Father in heaven, hallowed be Your name. Your kingdom come. Your will be done on earth as it is in heaven...."* Worship is happening around God's throne continuously, and it should be happening around the clock in our lives as well. And it can be when we walk in the revelation knowledge about worship.

I often hear myself during times of deep intercession cry out these words of worship, *"Holy, holy, holy is the Lord God Almighty, who was, who is, and who is to come."* And there are times I will declare these words of worship over and over again, not in vain repetition do I say these words, but with faith. These words of worship are declared in the third heaven by the four living creatures and bring great comfort to me knowing that our God has always been, and is, and will always be the Great I AM. Hebrews 13:15 teaches us of a continual sacrifice. Let's read about this from the New Living Translation of the Bible: *"Therefore, let us offer through Jesus a continual sacrifice of praise to God, proclaiming our allegiance to his name."*

When I break into this type of intimate worship, whether I am by myself or with a group, while declaring His greatness I can't help but fall to my knees in another dimension of worship like the twenty-four elders do when they hear the four living creatures cry out about God's supremacy. It's almost as if this type of worship weakens the knees of the created beings—us—as we come into the presence of our Creator. The Hebrew meaning of this type of worship is found in Strong's #1288 and is the word *barak,* which means to bless and to kneel.[2] In this realm of worship we literally fall to our knees and bless the Lord with words of praise and adoration.

A Life-Expression of Worship

Am I suggesting to you here that we are to worship the Lord 24/7 like these four living creatures around the throne? I guess I am, but perhaps not in the way you think I am. I am not suggesting that we put on a religious spirit and become legalistic about how we worship—rather that we get real with God and authentic with our worship. I don't believe we are to separate our worship from our daily living. Our lives need to become a living expression of worship to God.

Am I demeaning the action of vocalizing our worship to God—certainly not! But I am expanding upon the idea that our worship is to be more than mere words spoken, as heartfelt as they may be. We need to extend our worship into our daily lives and actually live in such a way that glorifies and pleases our Lord.

Allow me to make a comparison between these four living creatures and us. And yes, they are unique in their design, having six wings, and full of eyes around and within. But even though they are a unique creation group, even among themselves they have their created differences: the first one has the appearance of a lion; the second appears as a calf; the third has the face of a human; and the fourth is like a flying eagle. They are positioned to a specific region—around the throne—and their purpose is to worship. Despite their distinct features, they may be created more like us than we think.

As far as creation is concerned, God created us to be unique too, we are the only created beings designed in His image: *"So God created man in His own image; in the image of God He created him; male and female He created them"* (Genesis 1:27). We have been positioned in a specific region: *"And He has made from one blood every nation of men to dwell on all the face of the earth, and has determined their preappointed times and the boundaries of their dwellings"* (Acts 17:26). And not only are we unique in our design and positioned to a specific region, we are also created with a special purpose in mind: *"'For I know the plans and thoughts that I have for you,' says the Lord, 'plans for peace and well-being and not for disaster, to give you a future and a hope'"* (Jeremiah 29:11 AMP).

How do we do this? How do we make our lives an expression of worship twenty-four hours a day, seven days a week for the rest of our days on earth, especially during such unsettling times like now? Let me propose a very loose plan, and you fill in all the details; after all, it's your life to live and your expression of worship to give to God.

"Therefore, whether you eat or drink, or whatever you do, do all to the glory of God" (1 Corinthians 10:31). In other words, if you are a husband, become the best husband you can be and love your wife like Jesus loves the Church. You lay down your life for her. You are faithful and have eyes only for her. You build her up and encourage her. You protect her from anyone who wishes her harm. And you see to it that her daily needs are met. When you do these things, you follow the example of our Lord well.

If you are a mother, raise your children up in the ways of the Lord. Don't just tell them, but show them by your daily example what it means to be a Christian. Allow them to see and hear you read the Word. Teach the lessons of the Bible to them. You may miss it from time to time, but when you do, be the first to demonstrate the power of forgiveness and ask them to forgive you first, and help them do the same. Make sure they are well equipped with the fruit of the Spirit: love, joy, peace, long-suffering (patience), kindness, goodness, faithfulness, gentleness, and self-control (see Galatians 5:22-23). You do well in the mothering of your children when you raise them in the ways of the Lord.

If you call yourself a lawyer, then be a godly one and allow justice to prevail in every case that is presented to you. Care more about the well-being of your clients than you do about feathering your pockets. And make sure they know that you are not just a lawyer, but a Christian lawyer who is willing to pray with them for peace. And you, yourself, seek God on how to bring justice to the situation.

If called by God to be a pastor, feed the sheep, prepare them a hearty spiritual meal, tend to the lambs, watch over them, and see to it that they are growing in the things of God. Also know that if your own household is not in order, you are not prepared to stand behind that pulpit.

Perhaps you work in car sales? If so, be honest and sell people the best car you have for the most affordable deal you can give them. If something is wrong with the car, disclose that information to them. If it's a lemon of a vehicle, don't sell it. Let customers know you are a Christian who sells cars—build a reputable business, one that Jesus could sign His name to.

Oh, you're in politics? Humble yourself and serve the people who voted for you to represent them. Keep the law of the Lord in the center of your heart, which is to love God and to love your neighbor as you love yourself. Everything you do draws from your love for the Lord.

Whatever you do in this life, do it in such a way that it truly becomes an expression of worship.

> *Now may the God of peace who brought up our Lord Jesus from the dead, that great Shepherd of the sheep, through the blood of the everlasting covenant, make you complete in every good work to do His will, working in you what is well pleasing in His sight,*

through Jesus Christ, to whom be glory forever and ever. Amen (Hebrews 13:20-21).

Again, I do believe that worship is to be an expression of a life dedicated to God. If we will take action to implement these different forms of worship, not only will we worship Him in spirit and in truth, but our lifestyle will transform into a 24/7 song that sings the praises of God.

Now that we have a better understanding about worship—that it isn't a weekly worship service, but is meant to be a life-expression—in the next chapter we turn our attention to contemplating what it means to plunge into the deep with Holy Spirit, and what we must do in these turbulent times to do so.

Prayer

Father God, I dedicate my lifestyle to You as an expression of worship. During fiery trials I keep my eyes true to You. I look to no other for help, because I know my help comes through You. You are the only One who is worthy of my praise. Whether with my words or actions, I worship You in spirit and in truth. In Your most holy name I pray, amen.

Faith Assignment

Your faith assignment for this chapter is to reread the message under the subtitle, Build Your Sanctuary for God. Give thought and consideration on how you will build your sanctuary, and begin to use it daily. Keep a record of thoughts, answered prayers, prophetic visions and utterances that take place each day. Review this record book often and begin to worship God for answered prayers.

Questions to Ponder and Answer for Chapter 2: A Life-Expression of Worship

1. Your life is to be what?

   _____

   _____

   _____

2. The Father is seeking those who will do what?

   _____

   _____

   _____

3. What does worship reflect?

   _____

   _____

   _____

4. Describe celebration worship.

   _____

   _____

   _____

5. List six steps to overcoming fiery hot situations.

   _____

   _____

   _____

6. What is a priest's role?

_____

_____

_____

7. Jesus made you a king unto God; what did He give you to fulfill this position?

_____

_____

_____

8. How do you build your personal sanctuary for God?

_____

_____

_____

9. What types of things can happen during corporate worship when guided by the Scriptures?

_____

_____

_____

10. How is worship happening around God's throne?

_____

_____

_____

11. What does *barak* mean?

_____

_____

_____

12. Where do you need to extend your worship?

_____

_____

_____

13. How do you make your life an expression of worship twenty-four hours a day, seven days a week for the rest of your days on earth, especially during unsettling times?

_____

_____

_____

Personal Assessment

Have I misunderstood worship in the past? Do I have a clearer understanding of it now? Did I know that I was a priest and a king unto God? Have I been fulfilling these spiritual positions in my life? Or do I need to make some changes to fulfill these callings? Have I built a sanctuary with my heart for the Lord? Do I enter into my sanctuary on a daily basis? Or do I need to be more dedicated? Have I allowed my life to be an expression of worship? If not, how might I change my life-expression to that of worship?

Group Discussion

As a group, discuss what it means to be a priest and a king unto God. Be honest and discuss how you feel about these callings? Talk about different positions in life and how we might better fulfill these positions so that we can worship God in every area of our lives, including our life professions. Together as a group, enter into warfare worship over a current cause that is negatively affecting your area, life, or country.

Notes

1. Strong's Hebrew Lexicon Number H1984; *hâlal;* https://studybible.info/strongs/H1984; accessed May 22, 2020.
2. Bible Hub; *barak;* https://biblehub.com/hebrew/1288.htm; accessed May 22, 2020.

3

Plunge Into the Deep Waters of Repentance

Word of the Lord

The Spirit of the Lord would say to you this day,

> *Allow Me to lead you into the deep waters with Me. Be not afraid of where I will lead you. I promise I will never leave you, nor forsake you. I promise to be with you, even to the ends of the earth. I desire to take you in the deep, hidden truths of My Spirit so I can use you to the full potential that I created you for in these latter days. But first I must take you to the deep waters of repentance. And for many it is a place you do not want to go, but it is where your deepest hurts and disappointments will be healed. And you will be loosed from your greatest fears that have you bound to the strongholds of the enemy. I say be not afraid, take hold of My hand, trust Me, for I desire to set you free.*

Where Does the Deep Begin With the Spirit?

Such excitement stirs within us when we allow ourselves to think about plunging into the deep and glorious realm of the Spirit. Our imaginations visualize great spiritual adventures of the supernatural kind such as dreams, visions, healings, heavenly visitations, and creative miracles.

And yes, all of these and so much more await us as we plunge into the deep with the Spirit.

But let's take a moment to contemplate what it means to plunge into the deep and glorious realm with Holy Spirit. Our uncontrolled mind and emotions throw us into the deepness of the Spirit instantly, but I'm telling you from experience it doesn't work this way. This is where it will eventually lead us to, but this is not where it begins. Before plunging into the deep and glorious, let's find out just where this supernatural realm begins.

In the natural, the beginning of the deep is at the bottom of the sea. And in the deepest part of the ocean, it's dark, the pressure is strong, it's unbreathable, and a lonely place to be.

But spiritually speaking, in order to go into the deep and glorious of the supernatural realm with God, we must start here. And even though we may feel like we are all alone in this place, we are not. The Spirit of the Lord is with us.

> *Where can I go from Your Spirit? Or where can I flee from Your presence? If I ascend into heaven, You are there; if I make my bed in hell, behold, You are there. If I take the wings of the morning, and dwell in the uttermost parts of the sea, even there Your hand shall lead me, and Your right hand shall hold me* (Psalm 139:7-10).

Spiritually speaking, the deep for us begins in the depths of repentance. This is not a popular topic in most pulpits nowadays. Many think they can rent a big hall, hire great-sounding musicians and singers, add a moving preacher who can preach, send out the invitations, and we've got ourselves a great revival. But that's not how it works. A true revival always starts with a repentant heart.

When we look at the great prophets of the Bible before they walked in the true power of the Spirit, they all went down into the depths of repentance. The closer they moved toward God, the more they sensed

His holiness and saw how unworthy they really were. They felt inadequate for the job and the need for a spiritual cleansing. In today's world, it's the same for us.

This was Isaiah's response when he entered into the presence of God and received the prophetic call,

> *So I said: "Woe is me, for I am undone! Because I am a man of unclean lips, and I dwell in the midst of a people of unclean lips; for my eyes have seen the King, the Lord of hosts"* (Isaiah 6:5).

You may feel like Isaiah did here—undone! This is the beginning of the second wave, but fear not. Instead, trust God to take you into the deep waters of repentance and have His way with you, cleansing your heart from all ungodliness.

Prophetic Dream—Repent Now!

The other week I had a prophetic dream about the necessity for repentance in these last days. In this dream my family and ministry assistant were inside a large two-story building. We were all on the upper level. As I looked around, I saw other people were with us, and I noticed that the building was round with large floor-to-ceiling windows. So no matter which direction I looked, I could see outside the building. As I continued surveying the situation, I saw many people outside.

The next thing I knew I was outside in the midst of the people, calling out to them to look up at a great storm, a tornado above us. It was about to hit, but something unseen was holding it back. I was trying with all my might to get the people to look up and see the killer storm that was going to wipe out everyone who was not inside the building.

Then some people in the crowd saw the great storm fast approaching, and they ran inside to the safety of the building.

I continued trying with all my might to tell the rest to get inside, and some listened and ran inside with me. And as soon as we made it into the building, the storm was loosed. The majority of the people did not heed the warning. Everything happened so fast; it was very frightening.

Once inside I heard my husband telling the people that they needed to bathe in the sauna. People were running inside to quickly bathe.

Then all of a sudden the storm hit hard outside the building and I saw people of all different races thrown against the outside of the window. They were in a standing position, but they were all dead.

I woke up in great fear from this dream and had to actually go into the living room to pray in the Spirit to calm myself down.

I knew the Lord was speaking to me, but what did this all mean?

This prophetic dream reminded me of a vision the Lord gave to me many years ago while I was ministering in Africa. But what I saw in Africa was a vision of an ark, but it was the same principle—whoever was inside was safe. The focus of this past vision was filled with warmth and comfort. But this recent prophetic dream was filled with death for the multitudes who refused to listen and run for their lives to the safety of the building. The timing in this dream for the people caught outside meant imminent death for them.

The large tall windows that went around the building represented a clear message for all to see. The great storm, the deadly tornado that was upon us would not only release death, but a state of chaos and confusion upon the earth. The urgency in my message was calling out to the people that their time was short, get ready, get inside the safety of the blood covenant with the Father through the redemptive blood of Jesus Christ.

Why did the people in the dream have to take a sauna as soon as they entered the building? Because they were spiritually dirty and needed to rid themselves of all their spots and wrinkles. The only way to do this is by repentance.

> *Let us draw near with a true heart in full assurance of faith,*
> *having our hearts sprinkled from an evil conscience and our*
> *bodies washed with pure water* (Hebrews 10:22).

The multitude of dead people who slammed against the windows were those who would not heed the warnings of the Lord. The storm came and it was too late for them. It killed them and they could not enter in, even though the message was clear—repent.

And the message to us in this prophetic dream is clear: the time is short, get ready, make sure our hearts are pure from sin before it is too late.

> *From that time Jesus began to preach and say, "Repent [change*
> *your inner self—your old way of thinking, regret past sins, live*
> *your life in a way that proves repentance; seek God's purpose*
> *for your life], for the kingdom of heaven is at hand"* (Matthew
> 4:17 AMP).

Sin Is Being Judged—Prophetic Vision

Very recently the Lord gave me a prophetic vision while in prayer with my ministry assistant. In this vision I was looking down from above into a courtroom that was filled with many lawyers who were examining a book with handwritten entries of sins (wrong doings). I saw that this book was sitting on top of a much larger, weightier book. I then saw that this larger book was the Holy Scriptures, the Bible. I knew in my spirit that these wrong doings were being judged by the Supreme Judge, God Himself whom I saw in the front and center of all that was going on in this court of law. The sins that were written down were being judged according to the Scriptures.

How Are Sins Judged?

As Christians we know that the judgment for the sins of the unbeliever leads to eternal hell and damnation. Revelation 20:15 makes it plain for all to see, *"And anyone not found written in the Book of Life was cast into the lake of fire."* Their greatest sin is that they rejected the salvation of the Lord.

But you might be wondering, *How are the sins of the believer in Jesus Christ judged?* Good news for the true follower of Christ. Our confessed sins are covered and paid in full by the redemptive blood of Jesus Christ. This is something to shout about! We do not need to be fearful and worry because according to First John 1:9, *"If we confess our sins, He is faithful and just to forgive us our sins and to cleanse us from all unrighteousness."*

It was the sins of the unbelievers being judged in this vision, along with the unrepented sins of the believer. First Peter 4:17 tells us, *"For the time has come for judgment to begin at the house of God; and if it begins with us first, what will be the end of those who do not obey the gospel of God?"* And this is where we are going to focus our attention—the sins of the Church.

What does the Bible have to say about sin, sickness, and death? In Deuteronomy 28:15 it says:

> But it shall come to pass, if you do not obey the voice of the Lord your God, to observe carefully all His commandments and His statutes which I command you today, that all these curses will come upon you and overtake you.

Now let's turn to the New Testament in Romans 6:23 and find out if this still applies today. It clearly states that, *"For the wages of sin is death, but the gift of God is eternal life in Christ Jesus our Lord."* Disobedience and sin are one and the same; they open the doors of our lives to their consequences—sickness, disease, death, and all other forms of the curse.

Sin is increasing in these last days, and it seems to be taking on much deeper tones of evil than most of us care to hear about. It has even been running rampant in the Church; and this sin is being judged. It has to be dealt with because Jesus is returning for a Church that is without spot or wrinkle.

> *Husbands, love your wives, just as Christ also loved the church and gave Himself for her, that He might sanctify and cleanse her with the washing of water by the word, that He might present her to Himself a glorious church, not having spot or wrinkle or any such thing, but that she should be holy and without blemish* (Ephesians 5:25-27).

During recent healing seminars and conferences, I witnessed the Holy Spirit dealing with grave sin issues in the healing lines. Both men and women openly repented of sin issues that had them bound to a spirit of death that I talk about in my book, *Conquering the Spirit of Death*.

This may not be a pleasant topic, but it is necessary to confront. We the Church have been placed in this world for a purpose, God's purpose to be a witness and win them to the Lord. We were not meant to conform to their worldly, sinful ways.

Without Spot or Wrinkle

How does the Lord urge His people to prepare for His return? He tells us to look inward and judge ourselves, and in doing so we will not be chastised by Him. Ephesians 5:26-27 (AMP) says:

> *So that He might sanctify the church, having cleansed her by the washing of water with the word [of God], so that [in turn] He might present the church to Himself in glorious splendor, without spot or wrinkle or any such thing; but that she would be holy [set apart for God] and blameless.*

Just as a bride makes herself ready for her groom on the day of her wedding, so we prepare ourselves for this great and glorious reunion with our most precious groom—Jesus Christ.

How do we present ourselves to our Lord without spot or wrinkle? By washing the spots, the sin issues in our own lives with the Word of God. The message of redemption is based on the all-powerful blood of Jesus. We need to look into ourselves and in all honesty repent of any and all wickedness. And what is this wickedness? It is anything going against the ways of our Lord found throughout the Scriptures.

And we need to rid ourselves of the wrinkle. The wrinkle is the old self, the sinful nature that died when we believed in our hearts and confessed with our mouths that Jesus is Lord. But the flesh wants to resurrect the old self, so that it continues living in the same old nature. Even though we need to work out our salvation on a daily basis, our God always has a better plan. We die to the sinful nature and rise up with a recreated spirit in Christ—where past sins are forgiven and forgotten and we are given a brand-new beginning, a fresh start in life.

> *Therefore, if anyone is in Christ, the new creation has come.*
> *The old has gone, the new is here!* (2 Corinthians 5:17 NIV)

Let's turn our attention now to areas that we need to repent of that are hindering us spiritually from moving in the power of His might during turbulent times.

Repent from the Sin of Compromise

Compromise is a sin, and it is also spiritual suicide. This is how our enemy, satan and his demon, the spirit of death, come after us to steal, kill, and destroy our eternal relationship with our Lord Jesus Christ.

When we compromise, we lower or weaken our standards. And for Christians, God's Word, the Holy Bible, is our standard. The Bible is God's book of rules and regulations for how we are to live life on earth.

It teaches us spiritual boundaries for healthy living in spirit, soul (mind and emotions), and with our physical bodies as well. And when we obey His Word, we walk in His blessings; and when we choose not to obey, we walk in the consequences of our willful disobedience.

Let's face it, in these last days, God's people are being pressured by a lost society to compromise God's ways. But as disciples of Christ should we allow society to dictate our beliefs and convictions? No. What does the Bible have to say to us concerning compromise? *"If anyone, then, knows the good they ought to do and doesn't do it, it is sin for them"* (James 4:17).

And why do many of God's people compromise, lower, or weaken their standards today? Because they are fearful of what might happen if they take a stand for God's righteousness. What are some of the things they fear? They fear losing their position, title, job, finances, possessions, popularity, friends, and the list goes on and on. But according to the Bible, we are not to fear these earthly matters; rather we are to cherish the eternal ones that matter:

> *For if we go on willfully and deliberately sinning after receiving the knowledge of the truth, there no longer remains a sacrifice [to atone] for our sins [that is, no further offering to anticipate], but a kind of awful and terrifying expectation of [divine] judgment and the fury of a fire and burning wrath which will consume the adversaries [those who put themselves in opposition to God]* (Hebrews 10:26-27 AMP).

Have we taken the time to weigh the outcome of compromise? Do we really want to put ourselves in opposition to our God? What happens when we do?

> *Anyone who has ignored and set aside the Law of Moses is put to death without mercy on the testimony of two or three witnesses. How much greater punishment do you think he will deserve*

who has rejected and trampled underfoot the Son of God, and has considered unclean and common the blood of the covenant that sanctified him, and has insulted the Spirit of grace [who imparts the unmerited favor and blessing of God]? For we know Him who said, "Vengeance is Mine [retribution and the deliverance of justice rest with Me], I will repay [the wrongdoer]." And again, "The Lord will judge His people." It is a fearful and terrifying thing to fall into the hands of the living God [incurring His judgment and wrath] (Hebrews 10:28-31 AMP).

We are created to be more than conquerors and win every battle we face. And not only battles against physical death, but also spiritual death that comes to us by way of compromise.

Yet in all these things we are more than conquerors through Him who loved us (Romans 8:37).

Along with repentance, what steps can you take to overcome the sin of compromise?

1. Rededicate your life to Jesus, not just as Savior—make Him your Lord.
2. Renew ways to refresh your mind with the Word of God.
3. Study the Book of Proverbs to build godly character traits.
4. Develop true relationship with God the Father, Jesus, and Holy Spirit.
5. Examine your present lifestyle and make the necessary adjustments to protect your walk with the Lord.

Prayer of Repentance

Father God, I have fallen from Your grace. I have literally trampled upon this supernatural power that Your love and mercy purchased to redeem me from the sin of compromise. I choose this day to allow my faith to burn hot for you and never more to be lukewarm toward You and Your ways. Help me, Holy Spirit, to redeem the time I have lost for Your glory in my life, amen.

The Sin of Holding on to a Familiar Spirit

Holding on to a familiar spirit is sinful and something of which we need to confront and repent. You may be wondering, *Just what is a "familiar spirit"?* How does it affect our health and hinder our well-being? How does it gain access into our being? And how do we get free from it?

First of all, what is a familiar spirit? It's a demon, an evil spirit bent on our destruction. It takes its orders from satan, whose only desire is to steal from us, kill us any way possible, and to destroy us and all that is important to us.

Jesus says in John 10:10 about our enemy, the devil, *"The thief does not come except to steal, and to kill, and to destroy. I have come that they may have life, and that they may have it more abundantly."*

When we hear the word *familiar* we hear the word *family*. And this is what happens, this familiar spirit becomes like a family member and gains personal access into every area of our lives.

Allow me to give you some spiritual insight I have gained over the past twenty-five years ministering healing to people. I believe you will see clearly how a familiar spirit stops your healing from manifesting and/or hinders your well-being. This message will help you to recognize what's keeping you sick and weak, and steps to take to get free from this familiar spirit.

When you are bound to a familiar spirit, these are the signs when it comes to sickness and disease or a negative situation, such as an addiction:

- The disease or the problem is the center of your entire life.
- Your every conversation revolves around this sickness.

- Quite frankly, you wouldn't even know what to say if you didn't talk about it.
- You know this disease inside and out.
- You are very "familiar" with it.
- You know it better than you know your spouse, your kids, the Bible, even God Himself.
- It has become your closest family member.
- It even becomes your idol, your god.
- Your very life and conversations are consumed with it.
- You don't do anything without consulting the disease first.
- It totally controls your every moment.

Ways a Familiar Spirit Gains Entrance

The following are a few ways a familiar spirit gains entrance into a human's being:

- Sometimes, a familiar spirit enters through a generational curse such as breast cancer passed down from one family member to another.
- "Soul ties" is another way a familiar spirit is transferred to you, which is through sexual relationships. What has the other person bound will bind itself to you.
- A transferring of spirits from people you are around a lot, like a spiritually unhealthy friend, coworker, school professor. You pick up their unhealthy forms of speech and ways of thinking.
- Also, the transferring of spirits can take place in a spiritually polluted atmosphere like bars and hotel rooms, or by watching ungodly shows, such as a horror movie. While watching a horror show, a spirit of fear enters you and takes control of your mind and emotions.

- Reading ungodly materials is another way that a transferring of spirits can happen; for example, you look through pornographic magazines or websites and you may quickly find yourself in bondage to a porn addiction.

- A familiar spirit also gains entrance into our beings via the supernatural power of our own words. Always remember what it says in Proverbs 18:21 (AMP), *"Death and life are in the power of the tongue, and those who love it and indulge it will eat its fruit and bear the consequences of their words."* A good example of this is if you continually say you're poor; you end up cursing your finances and hindering God's financial supply over you and your family.

Freedom From a Familiar Spirit

There are three ways to gain freedom from a familiar spirit:

1. Renounce the familiar spirit.
2. Repent to God for allowing its entrance in your life.
3. Release yourself from it.

Renounce

The word *renounce* means "to cast off or reject, as a connection or possession; to forsake; as, to renounce the world and all its cares."[1] So, when I renounce this familiar spirit I cast it off and break its connection with me.

Command aloud, not shouting, but with authority,

In the name of Jesus I renounce this familiar spirit. I command it out of my being in the name of the Lord Jesus Christ.

Repent

Repent to the Lord for allowing a familiar spirit entrance into your life. Pray,

Father God, forgive me for allowing myself to speak negative word curses over myself, for not heeding godly counsel and hanging out with ungodly friends, for not speaking up against ungodliness with my coworkers, for not taking a stand against the teachings of ungodly professors, and for watching movies or reading materials that are destructive to my well-being, in the name of Jesus. Forgive me and help me to start afresh from this moment forward, amen.

Release

Release the healing and prophetic power of your words over yourself and pray this declaration prayer by the redemptive power of the blood of Jesus:

I am healed. I am delivered from this familiar spirit, and all other spirits that have latched on to the demon that is controlling my every thought and action. No longer will I allow this familiar spirit to control me. From this day forward, I will no longer familiarize myself with this disease or problem. I will become intimate with my heavenly Father, my Savior, Jesus Christ, and with my Comforter, Holy Spirit. I take up the Word of God, the Holy Bible, and I renew my mind and emotions with the promises of God. And in His precious name, I move forward free, strengthened, and healed in spirit, soul, and physical body, Amen and amen.

The Sin of Entitlement

The sin of entitlement is running rampant in the earth today. People who are bound to this sin are lovers of themselves and have an unbalanced absorption of self. Along with being egotistical and self-centered, they are impatient and demanding of others, thinking that everyone owes them everything for nothing. Their thoughts and words are a dead giveaway to their negative nature. They are the takers, never the givers.

Second Timothy 3:1-5 forewarns us about what it will be like in the last days:

> *But know this, that in the last days perilous times will come: For men will be lovers of themselves, lovers of money, boasters, proud, blasphemers, disobedient to parents, unthankful, unholy, unloving, unforgiving, slanderers, without self-control, brutal, despisers of good, traitors, headstrong, haughty, lovers of pleasure rather than lovers of God, having a form of godliness but denying its power. And from such people turn away!*

God provides for our every need; and yet, if we fail to guard our hearts and minds, we can become like the world and fall into this sin of entitlement. We can allow our thoughts and confessions to be filled with negativity and self-centeredness too. How do we break free from this sin of entitlement? The following seven principles give you the keys:

1. Admit that you have a problem with being self-centered.

2. After admitting that you struggle with the sin of entitlement, pray a prayer repentance, and ask for God's forgiveness.

3. With the help of Holy Spirit, our spiritual Teacher in life, learn to curb the immature desire to whine and complain and have it all your way.

4. Pay attention to your thoughts and stop the natural pattern of negativity.

5. When a negative thought comes to your mind, stop it, and say, "No! I'm not going to think like this." And instead of cursing the person with a negative thought, be creative and bless them aloud instead.

6. If you are in a struggle to complain about what you don't have, purpose in your heart to be a thankful person, first to God and then to others.

7. Be deliberate and put the needs and wants of others before yourself.

These seven principles, when put into practice, will help you to eradicate the sin of entitlement in your life.

A Prayer of Repentance

Father God, forgive me for my selfish ways. I have become so self-centered and immature. I have lost my way in my walk with You. I ask for a fresh start today, to honor You first and to love others as You command. Instead of having to be served, help me, Holy Spirit, to learn to be a servant, like my Savior, Jesus Christ, no longer demanding my way, but submitting to Your way. I thank You by faith for the transformation that can take place. In Your precious name, I pray, amen.

The Sin of Pride

Let's look at another sin that needs to be addressed—the sin of pride. Whether inside or outside the Church, it exists, and God's people need to repent of it. I guess we tend to forget that our anointing comes from God, and without Him we can do nothing. This extraordinary healing power is His power working in and through us—not because of us.

There are many gifted pastors and ministry and worship leaders who are blessed by God for His glory, but have fallen because of the sin of pride. Well-known names probably come to your mind. Too quickly we can lose track of God's glory and focus on our own self-importance—we become too big for our spiritual britches. No matter what our position in God's Church, this level of pride is a stench in

His nostrils. We become so earthly minded and independent from God, that we forget our focus is to be Kingdom minded and dependent on Him alone.

The catastrophic worldwide events in 2020 have turned the tide of pride and many of God's people see how far they have fallen away from Him and their need to repent from this sin of pride. And if anyone still fights with the sin of pride, we need to repent of this wickedness at once. Let's remind ourselves, we are created in His image, but we are *not* the image. God is the One we reflect. We might be able to lead people to God and help them in many ways, but we cannot save them—only Jesus can.

Paul the apostle and coauthor Timothy address this issue in Philippians 2:3 (AMP), written to the Christian church in Philippi. They write under the anointing of Holy Spirit:

> *Do nothing from selfishness or empty conceit [through factional motives, or strife], but with [an attitude of] humility [being neither arrogant nor self-righteous], regard others as more important than yourselves.*

Matthew, a gift from God, writes to us in his book under the inspiration of the Spirit of God: *"In the same way, let your light shine before others, that they may see your good deeds and glorify your Father in heaven"* (Matthew 5:16 NIV).

Steps to take to turn away from the sin of pride:

1. Pray for forgiveness.
2. Turn away from selfishness.
3. Look for ways to meet the needs of others.
4. Don't think of yourself greater than you really are.
5. Appreciate the gifts and talents of others.
6. Do what you do for God's glory, not yours.

A Prayer of Repentance

Father God, in Your most holy name I come before You and repent for the stench that I have become to You because of the sin of pride. You know I did not intend for it to be like this. I confess I got caught up in the earthly realm and forgot who I was serving. Instead of serving You, I have been serving myself. I pray for Your forgiveness and for a fresh start in these last days. I so want to please You, Father. Whatever it takes, even if it means stepping down and someone else stepping in position—so be it. I realize that my witness has led people to emptiness and destruction. In Your great mercy, revisit them and lead them into the truth about Your great gift of salvation and love—Your Son, Jesus, made that possible. I humble myself before Your great greatness, and I choose to begin again. In Your most holy name, I pray, amen and amen.

The Sin of Abortion

Within the Body of Christ, abortion has become controversial—it shouldn't be, but it is. Many of God's people are living like the world and having sexual relations outside of marriage and causing unplanned pregnancies. Because of fear, shame, and selfishness, God's people are aborting their children.

You may think abortion is an easy way out and nobody needs to know, but God knows and you know. And the enemy, the devil knows and will torment you day in and day out for the rest of your life with the memory of what you have done.

If you are in this decision-making situation right now or in the future, God will walk you through it and show you whether you are to keep and raise your child or release your little one to an adoptive family.

Galatians 6:7 (AMP) warns us, *"Do not be deceived, God is not mocked [He will not allow Himself to be ridiculed, nor treated with contempt nor allow His precepts to be scornfully set aside]; for whatever a man sows, this and this only is what he will reap."* It's time to judge ourselves. What have we been sowing? That's what we are reaping. And not only our nation, but the world in general has been sowing very sinful acts that lead to death by the biblical principle of sowing and reaping. A prime example of this is abortion.

Abortion is a grave sin. It's one of the seven sins God hates the most. Proverbs 6:16-19 lists seven sins that God hates more than other sins.

> *These six things the Lord hates, yes, seven are an abomination to Him:*
>
> *A proud look,*
>
> *A lying tongue,*
>
> *Hands that shed innocent blood,*
>
> *A heart that devises wicked plans,*
>
> *Feet that are swift in running to evil,*
>
> *A false witness who speaks lies,*
>
> *And one who sows discord among brethren.*

Abortion is the shedding of innocent blood. And if you sow into this sin of death—abortion—you will also reap death. Somewhere, somehow this crop of death of the innocent will show up in your life.

The earth is saturated with the blood of aborted children, and their blood is crying out to God for justice. And the world is reaping what they have sown into. Many of God's people are reaping the consequences of this as well.

We need to repent of this murderous spirit and the sin of sacrificing our children's lives to the god of selfishness. Maybe you are too young to raise a child, then do what's right in the eyes of the Lord, give birth and choose adoption for the sake of your child. There are ministries to help you through the process.

Mercy and Healing from Abortion

It may be that you believed the lies, were overcome by the fears and already had that abortion, and you are suffering from the ill effects of guilt and shame. I want to extend a hand of compassion out to you and remind you that God's promise to forgive us of all unrighteousness is forever true. Reach out to Him today, give Him that deep inner wound, allow Him to forgive and heal you.

And this is not just a woman's issue, the man that has fathered and agreed to this abortion is just as guilty, and it is time for you to repent for not being there to raise your child, or to support the woman that was the mother of your child. It's time for you to own up to your part of this sin and make things right between you and Father God. It takes a heartfelt prayer of true repentance and you will be forever forgiven and free from this sin too.

Perhaps something unthinkable happened to you and you conceived because of rape or incest. Again, there are Christian ministries to help you and your child. Abortion will not heal the injustice, it only compounds the hurt and loss you are already experiencing. But God will help you to heal with the adoption process.

We need to humbly seek the Lord and pray for a revival of repentance to flow throughout the earth starting today. Second Chronicles 7:14 gives us a plan to heal our nations: *"If My people who are called by My name will humble themselves, and pray and seek My face, and turn from their wicked ways, then I will hear from heaven, and will forgive their sin and heal their land."* It's not enough to pray and seek God, we also have to turn from ungodly ways. When we do, He will hear from Heaven and forgive us of our sin and heal our land.

And may it be perfectly clear that even voting for candidates who stand for abortion is wrong. You become just as guilty as if you personally had an abortion. Many of God's people have partaken of this sin of abortion. This is very serious as we reap what we sow, if we sow into death we will also reap death. Our nation is in dire need of deliverance from a spirit of death, and the only pathway for this deliverance is through repentance.

Prayer of Repentance

Father God, I must confess this abortion from my past for what it is—sin. I ask for Your forgiveness. It was wrong, but I can't change the past. But I want to rewrite today and my future with Your redeeming blood to heal me spiritually. I no longer desire for there to be a hindrance between You and me. I need Your mercy to heal and cleanse my mind and emotions. I struggle with guilt and shame, and am haunted by the bad memories of that grave day when I took the life of my baby. I need Your healing power to cleanse me from the pain and despair that I carry. I also need deliverance from the spirit of death that entered into my life that day. I break the generational curse that I caused over my future generations by the power of Your forgiving love and grace, in Your most holy name I pray, amen.

The Sin of Racism

What do most people do when they see a rat in their home? They get rid of it! Some may jump on a chair in fear for a while, but eventually they have to climb down off that chair, catch it, and dispose of it. On the other hand, others more daring may charge after the rat with a broom and chase it down until they trap it in a corner. Then there are those who are downright fearless and will go after the rat, step on it, and smash it with their foot.

A racist spirit is like a rat in the room, and we must go after it and squash it under our foot. We should not be the ones standing on the chair calling for someone else to deal with it. We are all responsible and need to deal with this spiritual rat that racism is and not be afraid.

In Guatemala we had two cats. Oftentimes in the night when we were all asleep, the male cat would crawl in through the cat door with a little rat in its mouth and call out to our female cat. It was a very distinct meow, and the other cat would wake up instantly from a deep sleep and run down a long hallway as fast as it could to go and devour that rat alive.

I think Christians should be like our old cats in Guatemala—every time we hear a racist slur or witness a racist act, we take immediate action to eradicate it, not allowing that rat of racism within our midst. Rats are rodents that carry infectious germs and deadly diseases and are not to be tolerated around us. Christians need to speak up and take action against the spiritual rats of racism, but do so in the name of the Lord—with love.

Ephesians 4:14-16 says,

> *We should no longer be children, tossed to and fro and carried about with every wind of doctrine, by the trickery of men, in the cunning craftiness of deceitful plotting, but, **speaking the truth in love**, may grow up in all things into Him who is the head—Christ—from whom the whole body, joined and knit together by what every joint supplies, according to the effective working by which every part does its share, causes growth of the body for the edifying of itself in love.*

The level of the sinful weapon of racist hate launched against the entire human race from the hands of satan has caused an upheaval of division of grievous proportions. But God has given us an even greater supernatural weapon to overcome the power of hate—His love. And there is only one way to spread this love—share the Gospel of Jesus Christ to the lost and dying people around us.

The enemy likes to exploit ignorance. Hosea 4:6 says, *"My people are destroyed for lack of knowledge...."* So if the enemy can keep people distracted and focused on the racism rat, this ignorance can cause division, death, and destruction.

This leads us to wonder with all the challenges and opportunities for racial division, "Where is the voice of the Church?" As the Church, God's people, we are to be the leading voice on earth. We are the ones called to be poured-out vessels that release healing and deliverance to hurting people.

Perhaps because of fear, is the Church, the Body of Christ, like the one who jumped up on the chair screaming for someone else to come and remove the rat of racism? If so, why? Doesn't His Word tell us that God has not given us a spirit of fear, but instead has given us supernatural power, love, and a sound mind? (See 2 Timothy 1:7.)

If we are a voice, a representation of Christ, how should we address this issue with one another?

- Speak the truth in love. Job 33:3 (AMP) shows us how to speak, *"My words will express the uprightness of my heart, and my lips will speak what they know with utter sincerity."*

- Forgive one another. Colossians 3:13 (AMP) describes this process in such a beautiful way, *"Bearing graciously with one another, and willingly forgiving each other if one has a cause for complaint against another; just as the Lord has forgiven you, so should you forgive."*

- Be teachable, willing to listen and to receive correction. Hebrews 12:6 (AMP) talks about the love of the Lord and His correction, *"For the Lord disciplines and corrects those whom He loves, and He punishes every son whom He receives and welcomes [to His heart]."*

- Be willing to unite to work toward making necessary changes. Psalm 133:1 (AMP) has this to say about unity, *"Behold, how good and how pleasant it is for brothers to dwell together in unity!"*

I have many testimonies about how the power of God's love brought correction upon the Church to heal someone damaged done by a racist spirit. One such testimony brings me back to a time of about twenty years ago when I ministered in a local church in Tanzania, East Africa, at the end of a weeklong healing conference. We experienced a glorious time together in the presence of the Lord, hugging and holding hands, singing and dancing with all our might. We feasted on the healing Word and for receiving manifestations of healing and creative miracles. Little did we know we would soon see a powerful and unusual miracle that would take the people by surprise.

It was Sunday morning and we were going to the meeting place to begin the last service for that weekend—it was the grand finale.

After breakfast I stepped out of the local restaurant and there sitting outside the door was an elderly man who had been badly beaten by life. He was homeless, as many were in that area. It was obvious he had not bathed in a very long time. His clothes were tattered and torn, and he was wearing no shoes. When I noticed his bare feet I began to really see his battle scars. He was missing toes and fingers and bits of his ears. I realized that he had been a victim of leprosy. He wasn't contagious; these were old battle wounds from many years ago when he suffered from this demonic disease. He also suffered from mental illness—whether this was from another battle or because of the battle with leprosy, I did not know, but it was obvious this man carried great pain with the shame of rejection.

I remember extending my hand and greeting him with the local greeting that I had learned. He returned the kind gesture with shiny eyes and a joyful smile. As Jesus would do, I invited him to come to the service as my special guest. He accepted, and we walked to the church service.

As we walked into the meeting hall, me in a pretty dress, and he in his Sunday best—all that he had—we sat down and he was seated next to me. His miracle that day was to be accepted, not passed over. He was the preacher's invited guest of honor. He felt honored, and honor heals many wounds.

As the power of honor was healing this man's wounded heart, the Spirit was revealing something else to me. I looked around and noticed that the dust from the dirt floor had settled from last night's powerful time of worship and miracles. But no sooner had I sat down when I felt something ungodly and sinful begin to raise from the foundation of the leaders inside—a racist spirit. The people had to be delivered from it, and this man had to be healed from its wicked powers.

Yes, there were wicked powers within the foundation of this church. There was no doubt that some in attendance were thinking, *How dare this pastor even think to invite someone like that man into our church?* They felt superior over him because his physical appearance was different from their appearance. We forget that our outward appearance is not who we are, and that God creates all people as equals in Him.

We, the Church, are God's hospital, and we are to welcome and accept the lost and hurting people around us and bring them into the healing power of the love of God. As His ambassadors here on earth, how else can we heal unless we first accept and invite all people into our midst?

When a racist spirit exists within the Church, it's evil and unwelcome by God. We must loudly hear Him saying, "Enough is enough!" It's time to purge the Church worldwide of such a vile spirit. The basic needs of all people are that we feel loved and accepted for who we are, not rejected for our appearance, economic status, or level of education.

One of the things God hates is a divisive spirit (see Proverbs 6:19). And a racist spirit is one that divides. Scriptures warn us that a house divided against itself cannot stand (see Matthew 12:25). We, the people, the true Church cannot be divided on this issue. We must practice honor, respect and love for one another, and stand united in Christ.

Bowing our knees to evil will not cause transformation; however, bowing our knees in humility with a heart surrendered to Christ can bring about supernatural transformation. Blaming others or holding the sins of someone's ancestors against them will not redeem the past hurt and injustice. Only the blood of Jesus can bring healing and forgiveness.

If we choose to join with others to take action and protest against a racist spirit, let us do so in a peaceful and productive manner. Rioting and looting do not advance the cause for human equality; in fact, it sets the cause backward and ultimately fulfills the enemy's plan. This is actually one of the many traps the enemy often uses to hold people in bondage to a racist spirit.

Colossians 3:17 (AMP) instructs us concerning our words and actions: *"Whatever you do [no matter what it is] in word or deed, do everything in the name of the Lord Jesus [and in dependence on Him], giving thanks to God the Father through Him."*

About the importance of allowing our good works to shine before people, Matthew 5:16 (NIV) tells us: *"...let your light shine before others, that they may see your good deeds and glorify your Father in heaven."*

I have friends from all around the world, and we don't ignore our physical differences—instead, we celebrate them. We get personal with one another and talk about hardships and sufferings that we have had to endure. And as friends, we share our cultures and family histories with one another. We also dine together, laugh and cry together, sing and worship the Lord together.

In all of our differences, God has created a great tapestry of unity through His Word. For example, John 13:35 encourages us in the faith: *"By this all will know that you are My disciples, if you have love for one another."*

God created all people with very unique traits, so to make a statement such as, "God is color blind," is not true. He didn't design us with the same earth suit. Some are tall, others are short. Our facial features are different, the color of our hair, eyes, and skin are different. Even among the same nationality there are differences from one another. God made us so unique that no one else on earth has or will ever have your fingerprint!

While we notice one another's earth suits, we should celebrate our physical differences—never hold differences against anyone. To do so is being racist, which is evil, sinful, and must be repented of. First John 1:7 reiterates this ungodly attitude, *"But if we walk in the light as He is in the light, we have fellowship with one another, and the blood of Jesus Christ His son cleanses us from all sin."*

What I am saying here is that we must treat each other as we are— equals, accepting the truth that we are all created in the mirror image of the Father, Son, and Holy Spirit. Our physical differences shouldn't matter to us.

God set the stage for this foundational truth in Genesis 1:27, *"So God created man in His own image; in the image of God He created him; male and female He created them."* God is a Spirit being, and underneath our earth suits we too are spirit beings. In fact, this is who we really are, and we can choose what our spiritual being looks like to God. For instance, we can be good and kind, or we can be wicked and mean. We can be humble or prideful, peaceful or angry. We can have a giving nature or a selfish one. We can be faithful or unfaithful.

The point is that *we are what we choose to be.* This has nothing to do with where we were born, who our parents are, our level of education, financial situation, or what type of job we have. Who we are doesn't have a thing to do with natural circumstances, but what we decide to do with what we have spiritually.

As believers, God gives us spiritual gifts, and what we do with these gifts affects our lives in the natural and spiritual realms. Three of the basic spiritual gifts given to us by God are: free will, salvation, faith to believe.

1. **Free Will.** God has given us the power of a free will—and along with our free will comes great responsibility. The outcome of our life is a direct result of the choices we make. This is why it is so important we use our free will wisely and make wise choices. Galatians 6:7 (AMP) tells us, *"Do not be deceived, God is not mocked [He will not allow Himself to be ridiculed, nor treated with contempt nor allow His precepts to be scornfully set aside]; for whatever a man sows, this and this only is what he will reap."*

2. **Salvation.** With our gift of free will, we can choose to receive or reject God's plan of salvation. Romans 10:9 (AMP), tells us what we must do to be right with God: *"If you acknowledge and confess with your mouth that Jesus is Lord [recognizing His power, authority, and majesty as God], and believe in your heart that God raised Him from the dead, you will be saved."*

3. **Faith to believe.** Again, with the free will that we have been given we can choose to be responsible and act in faith by believing and trusting God. Mark 11:23 (AMP) explains: *"I assure you and most solemnly say to you, whoever says to this mountain, 'Be lifted up and thrown into the sea!' and does not doubt in his heart [in God's unlimited power], but believes that what he says is going to take place, it will be done for him [in accordance with God's will]."*

There are no limits to the good that can be accomplished by the supernatural power of your faith. And being created equal by God and endowed equally with these three gifts from God: free will, salvation, and faith to believe. We can all choose to be blessed and assured in the goodness of God both on this earthly realm and in eternity as well.

In acknowledging the sin of being racist against one another let's pray and ask the Father to forgive us.

> *Father God, we, the Body of Christ ask for Your forgiveness for allowing our physical differences to stand in the way of how we treat each other. Help us to see past our earth suits and see that we are all created in Your mirror image. And that we are all equally loved and endowed by spiritual gifts from You. We also repent for being passive Christians and not speaking up against a racist spirit, and for tolerating it in our midst.*
>
> *Holy Spirit, we ask for Your direction on how to heal all the damage that has been done between one another. And even though the world pitches this as an impossible situation, we know that with You all things are possible.*
>
> *Help us to recognize that when Jesus died on the Cross and shed His precious blood for our sins, He wanted us to know that all lives matter. Give us the grace to carry this same spirit as we interact with others in every area of our lives.*
>
> *In Your holy name, we pray, amen.*

The Sin of a Reprobate Mind

We need to repent before it's too late and we willfully turn ourselves over to the sin of a reprobate mind. You may be thinking to yourself, *I really don't understand what a reprobate mind is.* If this is you, you're not alone—many don't understand it because it's rarely taught from the pulpits today. Let's study the Scriptures to find answers.

Romans 1:28 from the King James Version of the Bible is where the phrase, "reprobate mind" is mentioned: *"And even as they did not like to retain God in their knowledge, God gave them over to a reprobate mind, to do those things which are not convenient."* I find that part of the confusion about this is that we no longer speak this way. I'm not sure if I ever heard someone use the word "reprobate," other than a Bible teacher or two.

The New King James Version of the Bible uses the phrase "debased mind," which means reduced in quality or value. Similar words would be *immoral* or *perverted.* As I continued to check out different versions of the Bible for this verse, I understood the Amplified version best: *"And since they did not see fit to acknowledge God or consider Him worth knowing [as their Creator], God gave them over to a depraved mind, to do things which are improper and repulsive."*

So what is a reprobate mind? According to Strong's G96, the Greek word is *adokimos.* And it means "not standing the test, or not approved." It also means "that which does not prove itself such as it ought, or unfit, unproved, or rejected."[2]

A Christian man who was called into ministry wrote me requesting prayer. He was fearful because even though there was a calling upon his life, he was addicted to pornography, which had been going on for many years.

He knew what he was doing was wrong, but year after year he made up excuses for his sin. Then one day he heard the Spirit of God say to him, "I am no longer going to tell you to stop." And many years later those words still haunt him.

He asked me the dreaded questions, "Have I been given up to a reprobate mind? Is it too late for me?"

What does God's Word call improper and repulsive and rejected by God? Let's read Romans 1:28-32 from the Amplified version of the Bible:

And since they did not see fit to acknowledge God or consider Him worth knowing [as their Creator], God gave them over to a depraved mind, to do things which are improper and repulsive, until they were filled (permeated, saturated) with every kind of unrighteousness, wickedness, greed, evil; full of envy, murder, strife, deceit, malice and mean-spiritedness. They are gossips [spreading rumors], slanderers, haters of God, insolent, arrogant, boastful, inventors [of new forms] of evil, disobedient and disrespectful to parents, without understanding, untrustworthy, unloving, unmerciful [without pity]. Although they know God's righteous decree and His judgment, that those who do such things deserve death, yet they not only do them, but they even [enthusiastically] approve and tolerate others who practice them.

The last verse of this Scripture passage really struck home to me, *"yet they not only do them, but they even [enthusiastically] approve and tolerate others who practice them."* The world is trying to force us into the tolerance movement. But should we tolerate what we know is against God and His Word? Certainly not! If we tolerate these ungodly practices we trade in our "mind of Christ" for a reprobate mind—one rejected by God! This is very dangerous territory.

I believe the Christian man who wrote in fear, worrying whether or not it was too late for him to repent, is grieving the loss of not fulfilling his calling. He feels shame for the sin of addiction to pornography. He is feeling sorrow and wants to repent. If he is ready to repent, it's not too late. But he is living in very dangerous territory, spiritually speaking.

A reprobate mind happens when the Spirit of God keeps coming to you and warning you to repent. But instead of heeding the command of the Lord, you make up excuses to hold on to your sin. You even blame others for your sin. You are taken over by sinful behavior. You are no longer just oppressed by the enemy, the devil, he is actually heavily pursuing you. And because you have willfully rejected God's repeated warning to repent, you have become possessed by the demon behind the sin. It takes control of you.

Steps to freedom—before it's too late:

1. Acknowledge you are in willful sin against God.
2. Stop blaming others or circumstances for your sin.
3. Ask God and others you have hurt to forgive you.
4. Acknowledge your sin to someone you trust.
5. Get Christian counseling.
6. Set up a system of accountability.
7. Renew your mind and emotions with the Word of God.

Prayer of Repentance

Father God, in Jesus' name, I cry out to You and admit I have disobeyed You. I have willfully sinned against You. I have hardened my heart toward You. No one else is to blame, only me. I ask for Your forgiveness. I cry out for deliverance from this demonic spirit that has been my god. I pray, Holy Spirit, for a fresh start this day. I pray for the strength to open up and admit to those I can trust that I need counseling and accountability. I pray for the healing and renewal of my mind. Help me, Holy Spirit, to redeem the time I have lost. May I live honorably for You from this day forward, amen.

How to Remain Free from Sin

When we have repented from the sins discussed in this chapter, how do we remain free from these and any other sin that has control over us?

Be diligent to study the Word of God. *"Be diligent to present your-self approved to God, a worker who does not need to be ashamed, rightly dividing the word of truth"* (2 Timothy 2:15). We are to stay planted in the Word of God, day and night. Joshua 1:8 (AMP) shows us how to do this: *"This Book of the Law shall not depart from your mouth, but you shall read [and meditate on] it day and night, so that you may be careful to do [everything] in accordance with all that is written in it; for then you will make your way prosperous, and then you will be successful."*

Five ways to activate your personal Bible study:

1. Read God's Word daily.
2. Think about what you've read throughout the day.
3. Confess Bible passages aloud to yourself.
4. Discuss with others what you are reading from God's Word.
5. Ask Holy Spirit how to apply God's Word to your life.

Develop a lifestyle of prayer. Your prayers, like your time spent in the Word of God, becomes a lifestyle. And your prayers are not to be vain repetitions, mindless words; prayer are to be meaningful, even rela-tional with your one and only true God. Openly communicate with Him because you remember He promises to never leave or forsake you. (See Deuteronomy 31:6.) So being mindful of His ever presence, make conversation with Him and consult Him first in all matters, big or small. Thank Him for all your blessings and acknowledge Him in all of your ways. (See Proverbs 3:5-6.)

Four ways to develop a lifestyle of prayer:

1. Be mindful of His presence and make conversation with Him throughout the entire day.
2. Do not pray with mindless words, but with meaningful words from your heart.

3. Consult with God first in all matters—both big and small.

4. When you are reminded of a blessing—thank Him for it.

Live like you believe, not compromising your beliefs to satisfy a lost and dying world that cannot begin to understand the ways of the Lord. Allow your light to shine in such a way that your good works glorify your heavenly Father. (See Matthew 5:16.) Your good deeds will draw on the hearts of the people around us to seek until they find what you have—right standing with the living God through the One and only way to salvation, Jesus Christ. (See Acts 4:12.) So live like you believe:

> But **be doers of the word**, and not hearers only, deceiving your-selves. For if anyone is a hearer of the word and not a doer, he is like a man observing his natural face in a mirror; for he observes himself, goes away, and immediately forgets what kind of man he was. But he who looks into the perfect law of liberty and continues in it, and is not a forgetful hearer but **a doer of the work,** this one **will be blessed** in what he does (James 1:22-25).

Three steps to live like you believe:

1. Do not compromise your beliefs.

2. Do what you do to please and honor God.

3. Don't just hear biblical teaching, do what it tells you to do.

The Blessing of a Sin-Free Lifestyle

An important part of living out your faith free from sin is displaying godliness, and there is a promise for the godly: *"But know that the Lord has set apart for Himself him who is godly; the Lord will hear when I call to Him"* (Psalm 4:3). The Lord is attentive and is listening for the call of the godly, faith-filled believer.

No matter how challenging it may be to overcome sin, it is worth the effort, not only to be free from demonic oppression or possession, but also to have the confidence that there is no longer a hindrance between you and the Lord.

There is an everlasting peace knowing wherever you are, no matter what is going on, whether big or small God's ear is always open to you. And at any given moment you are free to access Him and He will hear you call out to Him. This promise is a blessing to be cherished and to be sought after.

Prayer of Repentance

"Father God, I repent of the known sin issues that I have been struggling with in my life. Help me with the sins discussed in this chapter, the sins of compromise, entitlement, pride, and abortion so that I am not given over to a reprobate mind. I desire to be pleasing to You in every area of my life, and I don't want anything to stand in the way of our relationship. I want to be someone You set apart for Yourself. I want a direct line to Your ears. Help me, Holy Spirit, to develop godly character. In Your precious name, dear Jesus, I pray, Amen."

This has been a serious message to take in, but no doubt a necessary one for us to confront. In the next chapter you learn how to escape to higher ground during this supernatural tsunami wave of healing glory, and what four spiritual steps will take us to His higher ground.

Faith Assignment

One way to combat sin is to renew your mind with God's Word. So the faith assignment for this chapter is to read and study one chapter in Proverbs a day. If it is the first day of the month then read Proverbs 1. If it is the fifteenth day of the month then read Proverbs 15, or the thirtieth day of the month, read Proverbs 30—you get the picture. As you read through the chapter for the day, choose one verse that stands out to you, think about it, and if you can apply it to your daily life—do so.

Questions to Ponder and Answer for Chapter 3: Plunge into the Deep Waters of Repentance

1. In Ephesians 5:26-27, what does God want to do with the Church?

_____

_____

_____

2. The enemy uses the sin of compromise to destroy what?

_____

_____

_____

3. What does a familiar spirit gain?

_____

_____

_____

4. Explain the sin of entitlement.

_____

_____

_____

5. List six steps to help free us from the sin of pride.

_____

_____

_____

_____

_____

_____

6. In Second Chronicles 7:14, it's not enough to pray and seek God, I also have to do what?

_____

_____

_____

7. When you do as God says to do in Second Chronicles 7:14, what will He do?

_____

_____

_____

8. When it comes to racism, Christians need to be willing to do what?

_____

_____

_____

9. How should you speak up and take action against a racist spirit?

_____

_____

_____

10. What supernatural weapon has God has given you that is greater than the power of hate?

_____

_____

_____

11. What did God create all people with?

_____

_____

_____

12. How are you to treat each other?

_____

_____

_____

13. What are three basic spiritual gifts God has given you?

_____

_____

_____

14. Explain what a reprobate mind is according to Strong's G96.

_____

_____

_____

15. List the three ways given to activate your personal Bible study.

_____

_____

_____

16. In Psalm 4:3, what does God promise to do for those who are godly?

_____

_____

_____

Personal Assessment

How am I doing in the area of repentance? Am I holding on to pet sins? Am I compromising my faith? Am I clinging to the opinions of this world? Do I struggle with familiar spirits? How about with the sin of entitlement? Do I feel others owe me something for nothing? Am I struggling with a racist spirit? Do I really believe all people are created equal? Do I spend time in the Word daily? Do I pray every day? Am I living my life the way God wants me to? Am I being honest with myself in this personal assessment? If not, why?

Group Discussion

As a group of mature believers, discuss common areas in which Christians are compromising their faith. Pray together as a group for repentance for taking on the ways of this world rather than the ways of God. Take Holy Communion together. Afterward, discuss how to be free from sinful thoughts and actions.

Notes

1. *KJV Dictionary*, s.v. "renounce"; https://av1611.com/Kjp -dictionary/renounce.htm; accessed May 19, 2020.

2. *Blue Letter Bible*, "reprobate"; https://www.blueletterbible.org/lang/lexicon/lexicon.cfm?Strongs=G96&t=KJV, accessed May 15, 2020.

4

How to Escape to Higher Ground

Word of the Lord

The Spirit of the Lord God Jehovah would console you with these words this day,

> *My eyes are not blind, My ears are not deaf, nor are My hands withered toward you, My beloved Bride. I see and I hear all that is taking place around you, how the enemy is attacking the people of the earth, including you. Therefore, I am calling you to come up hither, escape to higher ground, bask in My presence of revelation truth and satisfy your weary soul. Embolden your faith this day, I pray and release the power of My eternal power to those in need around you. With these words I console you today.*

The warning is trumpeting throughout the whole earth, "Get ready, for the coming of the Lord is at hand." And yes, we have been hearing this warning for so many years now that our spiritual ears may have become dull and our hearts so unbelieving that many of us have not made the proper spiritual preparations. As the times are transitioning from "waiting to happen" to "suddenly taking place," these prophetic warnings have caught many of God's people off guard. And even though we have seen with our very own eyes supernatural events unraveling, we have chosen to walk around wearing spiritual blinders, refusing to accept what could possibly be unfolding around us.

But God does not wear spiritual blinders. He is well aware of all that is taking place. Even though He could rapture us up and out of these perilous times, He has not done so yet. And this should cause us to question, "Why?"

Knowing that nothing takes Him by surprise, He being the Omniscient One, knowing all things, past, present, and future, the next question we should ask ourselves is, "Do I trust Him enough to surrender all my fears and trepidations and accept that I am called by Him for such turbulent times as these?"

Prophetic Dream—Warning

During intercession the Lord continues to warn us about the chaotic times we have entered. The day before the Coronavirus/COVID-19 broke loose in the United States, God spoke to me in my dreams and said, *"Get ready, chaos is about to break out!"* And I woke up. The next day it broke out. You might wonder why He waited until the day before to give this warning. Actually, He had been warning me for a few months prior to that morning. He had been saying to prepare because chaos was soon to break forth.

Our family prayed and took steps to prepare the best we knew how. I also had shared with people who follow my teachings to do the same. But that morning, His warning in my dream was that chaos was imminent and to be ready now! He continues to caution us to make ourselves ready for the pressing times ahead.

Since the pandemic first appeared, chaos has been fueled by a spirit of fear that brought the world and its inhabitants to a standstill, causing an economic collapse. While people are panicked over a virus, global natural devastation is evidenced by extreme weather and events including: tornadoes, earthquakes, rain, flooding, out-of-control fires, and infestations of plagues such as killer wasps and crop-destroying locust spreading from one continent to another. And more destructive than all has been the increase of hate between the peoples of the earth. Hate crimes, hostile attitudes toward innocent people, looting and rioting, death and destruction surrounds us as the kingdom of darkness increases.

By God's amazing grace, we the Church are not defeated—we are called to be more than conquerors. Those who win a battle are prepared with a battle plan from God. Take note that when He gives the warning, *"Get ready, chaos is about to break out!"* He is not speaking about physical preparations—He is referring to spiritual preparedness for what is coming. And it is going to happen and is happening, whether we want to heed His warnings or not.

Five Spiritual Activities to Escape to Higher Ground

Let's face it, it's one thing to accept that God calls us for such times, but how do we begin to wrap our heads around the fact that our Messiah, the Omnipotent, all-powerful One who creates this universe, designs the power of the wind, water, gravity and all that holds this earth together actually needs us to be on earth at this time. A humbling thought to say the least—with His unlimited power, what could we possibly do for Him during these times?

I firmly believe we can escape to this higher ground of His by leaning into each of the following spiritual activities that will equip us, strengthen us, and give us the assurance we need from Him to be at peace while in the midst of chaos. Follow the leading of Holy Spirit, our Comforter, and do as He instructs: pray, raise the standard of the blood of Jesus, recognize the enemy, use the power of His name, and step into revelational truth.

1. Intercession

One of the main ways to escape the chaos and to head to higher ground is by intercession—by praying. Jesus shows Himself to be a man of prayer while on earth. By His true example we see how He keeps

Himself in tune with His heavenly Father and spiritually strong during stressful and demanding times—by praying routinely.

Disciple and physician Luke records accurate details of what he observed Jesus do. In Luke 5:16 we read one of his important details about our Messiah: *"So He Himself often withdrew into the wilderness and prayed."* If you ever wonder how many times we should pray, the answer by Luke's observation is "often." We should stop what we are doing and pray often throughout our daily business.

According to Mark 1:35 (NIV) we discover an interesting fact about when Jesus prayed: *"Very early in the morning, while it was still dark, Jesus got up, left the house and went off to a solitary place, where he prayed."* Knowing that details in the Bible are recorded for our benefit, getting up early in the morning to pray is a spiritual key to setting the events of the day in order.

Matthew, clearly a gift of the Lord to us, carefully documents the life of the Messiah for us to learn from. Matthew records this detail about the prayer life of Jesus Christ for us: *"And when He had sent the multitudes away, He went up on the mountain by Himself to pray. Now when evening came, He was alone there"* (Matthew 14:23). Something I know from personal experience is that ministering to the crowds can drain our strength, so it is important to spend time alone to deposit His supernatural strength back into us. Spending time alone with our heavenly Father at the end of the day revitalizes our spirit.

Yes, it is powerful to pray with others, but it is also important for our spiritual growth that we spend time alone praying to God. Jesus instructs us in Matthew 6:6:

> But you, when you pray, go into your room, and when you have
> shut your door, pray to your Father who is in the secret place;
> and your Father who sees in secret will reward you openly.

As we briefly observe the prayer life of Jesus in these four verses, we may think it is a lot of time to spend in prayer; but if we want to overcome in these turbulent times, we need to tap into this supernatural realm of intercession.

Even now in Heaven, Jesus remains in this all-powerful lifestyle of prayer. The apostle Paul writes to us in the Book of Romans, revealing this amazing insight about Christ's faithfulness toward us in prayer:

> *Who shall bring a charge against God's elect? It is God who justifies. Who is he who condemns? It is Christ who died, and furthermore is also risen, who is even at the right hand of God, who also makes intercession for us* (Romans 8:33-34).

You will note throughout this work is a strong emphasis on prayer and intercession. And the reason being is *prayer changes things.* The prayer of faith is a foundational move of Holy Spirit and accomplishes great things. As priests for God we must pray to be wired into His circuit of healing glory.

The following are eight areas to pray about:

1. ***The will of the Father be accomplished on earth.*** *"Your kingdom come. Your will be done on earth as it is in heaven"* (Matthew 6:10).

2. ***Pray for the forgiveness of sins for others.*** *"If anyone sees his brother sinning a sin which does not lead to death, he will ask, and He will give him life for those who commit sin not leading to death. There is sin leading to death. I do not say that he should pray about that"* (1 John 5:16).

3. ***Pray for your enemies.*** *"But I say to you, love your enemies, bless those who curse you, do good to those who hate you, and pray for those who spitefully use you and persecute you"* (Matthew 5:44).

4. ***Pray for protection from temptation.*** *"Watch and pray, lest you enter into temptation. The spirit indeed is willing, but the flesh is weak"* (Matthew 26:41).

5. ***Pray for the healing of others.*** *"Confess your sins to each other and pray for each other so that you may be healed. The prayer of a righteous person is powerful and effective"* (James 5:16 NIV).

6. ***Pray for our leaders.*** *"I urge, then, first of all, that petitions, prayers, intercession and thanksgiving be made for all people—for kings and all those in authority, that we may live peaceful and quiet lives in all godliness and holiness"* (1 Timothy 2:1-2 NIV).

7. ***Pray for the peace of Israel.*** *"Pray for the peace of Jerusalem: 'May they prosper who love you'"* (Psalm 122:6).

8. ***Pray in faith for your needs to be met.*** *"Therefore I say to you, whatever things you ask when you pray, believe that you receive them, and you will have them"* (Mark 11:24).

Granted, there are many things we can pray about, but this list of eight is a powerful start for your journey to higher ground.

2. *Raise the Standard of the Blood*

We have to admit that our enemy, satan, is lashing out with a vengeance against the entire human race. He is using weapons of fear laced with false reports and deadly acts against all people. These deadly attacks are coming at us in waves of fear, plagues and pestilence, hatred and murder, and so much more. People who are not spiritually aware of what is happening around them become easy prey for him to devour and destroy. This is why it is critical that we raise the standard of the blood of Jesus against the enemy—starting now!

Spiritually speaking, when we raise the standard of the blood, we elevate its power to a higher level of expectation. During these volatile times, we must deactivate mediocre faith and rise to a new level of unparalleled faith. A level of faith that makes the devil tremble with fear of his own failure, inadequacy, and lack of destructive power against us.

The prophet Isaiah declares to us this glorious promise of the protection of the Spirit of the Lord in our favor:

> *So shall they fear the name of the Lord from the west, and His glory from the rising of the sun; when the enemy comes in like a flood, the Spirit of the Lord will lift up a standard against him* (Isaiah 59:19).

3. *Recognize the Enemy*

Now more than ever before, we must realize that our attack is not against each other, but against the enemy and his kingdom of darkness. Paul, an apostle of Jesus Christ by the will of God, gives to us spiritual insight about the battles rising against us:

> *For we do not wrestle against flesh and blood, but against principalities, against powers, against the rulers of the darkness of this age, against spiritual hosts of wickedness in the heavenly places* (Ephesians 6:12).

The sooner we accept this fact, the quicker the victory will manifest for us. Why do I say this? Because when we know who and what we are fighting against, we will direct our efforts in the appropriate direction. And instead of fighting *against* one another, we will begin to fight *for* one another.

There are many reasons for these attacks against us, but I desire to mention two at this moment.

    1. The enemy's heart burns with hatred for us.

2. He knows that his time to steal, kill, and destroy us is short.

Be sober [well balanced and self-disciplined], be alert and cautious at all times. That enemy of yours, the devil, prowls around like a roaring lion [fiercely hungry], seeking someone to devour (1 Peter 5:8 AMP).

The thief does not come except to steal, and to kill, and to destroy... (John 10:10).

The devil is rabid and foaming at the mouth, just waiting for any opportunity to devour us. And he will if we let him, but we do not need to put up with his demonic nature—we can raise the standard of the blood against him and his wicked attacks. But we must remain sober, on the alert and cautious at all times.

Believers must activate authority and pray a declaration of faith against the enemy. Instead of him hunting us, we need to activate the powerful weapon given to us—the authority of Christ— and hunt down the enemy. With our spiritual authority, we have the right to order the enemy around and enforce obedience from him.

Jesus says to us in Luke 10:19, *"Behold, I give you the authority to trample on serpents and scorpions, and over all the power of the enemy, and nothing shall by any means hurt you."*

What would this look like? Say the enemy is attacking your community with a plague, you would activate your God-given authority over him and say, "Back off, devil! I have Christ's authority over you. And this plague may not enter into my household. I raise the standard of the blood, and this disease cannot survive on our hands, it cannot live in our bodies, and it cannot handle the pressure of the presence of Holy Spirit in me and my family. In the name of Jesus, I order you to leave, at once!"

Use the Power of His Name

There is no other name higher than the name of Jesus. And eventually every knee, whether human or spirit, will kneel before Him and confess that He is Lord. Wisdom beckons us to do so now, and not wait until it is too late. But unfortunately, many will wait until there is no longer hope for them for salvation—but glory to God this is not us; we believe in the saving grace of God and the sacrifice of Jesus.

We have been given the power of Jesus' name to use anytime, anyplace, and at will. His name is a weapon of warfare that when used by us, His disciples, backed with authority and faith, the enemy must surrender and walk away in defeat.

But instead of using this all-powerful name of our Savior and Lord when on the defense to fight off satan's already manifested attack, let us begin to use the name of Jesus on the offense, and attack him first. We will squelch many a battle before they begin if we put into effect this battle plan.

An example of this is with the physical health of our families. Instead of waiting for an attack of illness to come upon us, we can ward off the attack of sickness and disease beforehand with verbal confessions of faith, laced heavily with the all-powerful names, titles, and attributes of our Redeemer and Messiah—Yeshua. How might this look? We declare a simple confession of faith to speak aloud daily to build a wall of protection around ourselves and families that will help to keep the deadly attacks of sickness away from us, such as:

> *I partake of the Bread of Life this day and my physical body is strengthened. I drink of the Living Waters and my mind and emotions are refreshed. I call on my Deliverer who keeps me safe from pestilence and disease. I devour the Word of God and am healed in spirit, soul, and in my physical body, amen.*

Where do we find such names, titles, and attributes of our Lord? They are found throughout the Scriptures. Again and again, I express to you the importance of reading and studying the Bible. Let's read the verses where the four names from this confession of faith are found:

Bread of Life. *And Jesus said to them, "I am the bread of life. He who comes to Me shall never hunger, and he who believes in Me shall never thirst"* (John 6:35).

Living Waters. *Jesus answered and said to her, "If you knew the gift of God, and who it is who says to you, 'Give Me a drink,' you would have asked Him, and He would have given you living water'"* (John 4:10).

Deliverer. *"Wait for His Son from heaven, whom He raised from the dead, even Jesus who delivers us from the wrath to come"* (1 Thessalonians 1:10).

Word of God. *"He was clothed with a robe dipped in blood, and His name is called The Word of God"* (Revelation 19:13).

All-Powerful Names, Titles, and Attributes of Messiah to Call Upon

The following is a great list of names, titles, and attributes of the Lord Jesus you can use to implement your battle plan:

- Author and Perfecter of our faith (see Hebrews 12:2 AMP)
- Bridegroom (see Matthew 9:15)
- Chief Cornerstone (see Psalm 118:22)
- The Door (see John 10:9)
- Faithful and True (see Revelation 19:11)
- Gate for the sheep (see John 10:7-9 NIV)
- Good Shepherd (see John 10:14-15)
- King of kings (see Revelation 17:14)
- Light of the World (see John 8:12)

- Lord and Teacher (see John 13:14-15)
- Messiah and Christ (see John 4:25-26)
- Rock (1 Corinthians 10:4)
- Risen Lord (see 1 Corinthians 15:3-4)
- Savior (see Luke 2:11)
- Son of the Most High (see Luke 1:32 NIV)
- Victorious One (see Revelation 3:21 NIV)
- Vine (see John 15:5)
- The Way (see John 14:6)

The last four names come from the well-loved portion of Scripture, Isaiah 9:6 (NIV):

- Wonderful Counselor
- Mighty God
- Everlasting Father
- Prince of Peace

There are more names, but I believe this will be a blessing to add to your prayer time and confessions of faith.

The apostle Paul and bondservant of Christ writes to us in Philippians 2:9-11:

> *Therefore God also has highly exalted Him and given Him the name which is above every name, that at the name of Jesus every knee should bow, of those in heaven, and of those on earth, and of those under the earth, and that every tongue should confess that Jesus Christ is Lord, to the glory of God the Father.*

How might we use this plan of action against a spirit of fear? We could declare this way, "In the name of the Victorious One—Jesus Christ, the Author and Finisher of my Faith, by Your great power,

I will not give in to a spirit of fear. I command that this fear bows at the name of Jesus—my Deliverer, my Savior, and my Lord." Begin to declare praises to your Messiah—Yeshua. Speak, sing, and shout aloud the names of Jesus, over and over again, until you break off that stronghold of fear.

Step Into Revelational Truth

Many Christians seek supernatural encounters yet don't know what God's Word says. This is a risky mistake! Without the foundational truths from the Bible, we set ourselves up to be easy targets for deception. We forget that satan can appear as an angel of light (2 Corinthians 11:14). He and his demonic forces can easily change their skin to deceive even the elect if possible.

I cannot emphasize enough the importance for us to remain faithful to the study of the Word of God. Why do we think the enemy sends distraction our way when we decide to open our Bible to read and study from it? Because he is a lying spirit and is fearful of the truth and what will happen when God's truth is revealed to us. And if he, being evil, knows the power of God's Word, how much more should we recognize this truth. And not just recognize this truth, but turn the study of the Word into a lifestyle to be cherished, sought after, and lived to the best of our ability.

All too often we crowd our schedules with things that don't make a lasting difference in our lives. We fail to realize that our time in the Word can become a powerful time of direct fellowship with His Spirit. In the Bible is where Holy Spirit reveals life-changing truths that help to heal and set us free from the weight of the world. The more we know the Word, the more we understand who God is. As we mature in the faith, we become harder for the enemy to attack and deceive us.

Reading and studying the Holy Bible is a spiritual action that leads us to higher ground, and it is also the third wave in this supernatural tsunami wave of healing glory. The apostle Paul writes to his spiritual son, Timothy, while in prison, *"Be diligent to present yourself approved to God, a worker who does not need to be ashamed, rightly dividing the word of truth"* (2 Timothy 2:15).

Prayer

Dearest heavenly Father, just like my Messiah, I desire to head to higher ground with You when life around me becomes chaotic, rough, and even frightening. Holy Spirit, I ask that You work with me as I learn how to climb up to this mountaintop with You. Lead me during times of intercession and I pray in faith for the needs of my government, Israel, the needs of others, and for myself as well. Show me areas where I must raise up the standard of the blood of Christ in my life. Help me to remember to use the power of the name of Yeshua freely, not just in times of defense, but to also be on the offense with the enemy, the devil, and ward off his wicked attacks against me and my family. Teach me as I step into revelational truths in Your holy Word. I pray this all with confidence, amen.

In the next chapter we talk about the third wave in this tsunami wave of healing glory—revelational truth found in His Word—the Holy Bible. And take this message and preach the Word. We solidly affirm the importance in today's turbulent world to be ready in season and out of season to do so.

Faith Assignment

Furnish your personal sanctuary for the Lord with intercession and pray for your government leaders, for the peace of Israel, and for the healing of others around you for the next thirty days.

Questions to Ponder and Answer for Chapter 4: How to Escape to Higher Ground

1. What is the warning trumpeting throughout the whole earth?

     _____

     _____

     _____

2. What is one of the main ways to escape all the chaos and head to higher ground?

     _____

     _____

     _____

3. Spiritually speaking, what do you do when you raise the standard of the blood?

     _____

     _____

     _____

4. During these volatile times, what must you do?

     _____

     _____

     _____

5. According to Ephesians 6:12, you don't wrestle against flesh and blood. List what you wrestle against.

     _____

     _____

     _____

6. What are two reasons given for these spiritual attacks?

_____

_____

_____

7. You will squelch many a battle if you do what?

_____

_____

_____

8. Why does the enemy send distraction your way when you decide to open your Bible to read and study from it?

_____

_____

_____

Personal Assessment

As I meditate upon the teaching I have just read, where am I spiritually with all of this? Am I confident that I'm where I need to be, or do I lack in any of these areas: intercession, raise the standard of the blood, use the power of His name, and step into revelation truth found in the Word of God? If I see lack, what areas do I need to especially work on to grow in my faith? How might I go about preparing myself in these areas?

Group Discussion

Discuss as a group what areas of life you need to raise up the standard of the blood. What is happening in your community? Are there current issues you can intercede about? Do you believe that your times of intercession together will make a difference? How might you corporately use the power of the name of the Lord on the offense against your enemy the devil? Are you willing to intercede for your government, for the peace of Israel, and for the protection of the people in your community? And last but not least, are you willing as a group to step into revelational truth found in God's Word? Are you willing to take the message of the Word and implement its message into community situations? If so, come up with plans to do so.

5

God Expects Us to Preach the Truth

Word of the Lord

The Lord God would say to your heart this day,

> My children, be not afraid of the day in which you live. You have My promise that I will never leave you or forsake you. I have said that I will be with you even to the ends of the earth. I am faithful and true. And I the Lord God have called My people to be a voice for Me in the wilderness. I have given you an assignment to share the Gospel of Jesus Christ with all people. Everywhere you go now, open up your mouth and speak to everyone you meet. The time is here, and the time is now. Be ready to preach the uncompromised Word of the Lord to people who are stiff-necked and full of rebellion against Me and My ways. Speak what I say to speak. I am with you always. Thus says the Lord your God.

Our third wave in this tsunami wave of healing glory is a wave of revelational truth. And God has certain expectations for His Church with this wave. And one of these expectations is to preach the Word. According to Second Timothy 4:2-5 we are to be ready at all times to preach the Word of the Lord to people that no longer want to hear the truth. Now, this is a challenging assignment from the Lord. But if the

Lord asks us to do this, then there is a way to do so with great success that brings glory to the Lord.

Our End Time Assignment

In the midst of this chaos and great rebellion, we followers of the Son of the Most High are charged in Second Timothy 4:2-5 to:

> **Preach the word! Be ready in season and out of season. Convince, rebuke, exhort, with all longsuffering and teaching.** *For the time will come when they will not endure sound doctrine, but according to their own desires, because they have itching ears, they will heap up for themselves teachers; and they will turn their ears away from the truth, and be turned aside to fables. But you* **be watchful in all things, endure afflictions, do the work of an evangelist, fulfill your ministry.**

This is not a light-hearted assignment from the Lord; we have examples in the Word about the people of God who had messages to share that the people no longer wanted to hear. In Acts 7, Stephen delivers the Word of the Lord and the people did not like what he had to share. In fact, they were so displeased with the words of God that it says in verse 54, *"When they heard these things they were cut to the heart, and they gnashed at him with their teeth."* I don't know about you, but either I am very prophetic in nature or I have a vivid imagination, but just reading these words I can see and hear an angry mob just seething with hatred for the man of God like a pack of hungry wolves. And this rebellious wolf pack of men *"cried out with a loud voice, stopped their ears, and ran at him with one accord."* Then the crowd dragged him out of the city and murdered him with stones (see Acts 7:57-58).

And speaking of hungry wolves, we need to be well aware in these days that we are sheep gifted with grace sent out in the midst of hungry wolves. Matthew 10:16 warns us, *"Behold, I send you out as sheep in the midst of wolves. Therefore be wise as serpents and harmless as doves."* Even though we are sheep sent out in the middle of the wolf pack, we are not to be afraid. God has gifted us with His grace to win many people to Him during this end time battle. Hebrews 4:16 encourages us with these words of hope, *"Let us therefore come boldly to the throne of grace, that we may obtain mercy and find grace to help in time of need."*

As children of God we are gifted with His grace—we are clothed with His favor and blessing. We are clothed with His rich and royal robes of righteousness—His redemptive blood. We are given direct and instant access to Him anytime and anyplace. He promises to be with us always, even in the center of an angry mob like Stephen was. And even though he was martyred for his obedience and faith in his Messiah, something very amazing and supernatural happened and was actually recorded for our welfare and peace today.

Right before they began to attack Stephen, his spiritual eyes were opened into the prophetic realm:

> *But he, being full of the Holy Spirit, gazed into heaven and saw the glory of God, and Jesus standing at the right hand of God, and said, "Look! I see the heavens opened and the Son of Man standing at the right hand of God!"* (Acts 7:55-56)

Hebrews 4:16 (AMP), explains it this way for us:

> *Therefore let us [with privilege] approach the throne of grace [that is, the throne of God's gracious favor] with confidence and without fear, so that we may receive mercy [for our failures] and find [His amazing] grace to help in time of need [an appropriate blessing, coming just at the right moment].*

We are highly favored by God because of what Jesus did for us—He bled and died for us and rose from the dead. Because He chose to suffer for us, we can now come with all boldness and confidence and stand before His beautiful throne of grace and ask for His intervention in every situation.

At this point, your imagination may be running wild with fearful thoughts. You need to do as you are commanded right now in the name of Jesus, and take those negative thoughts and bring them under the submission of your faith and trust in your Deliverer and Savior. Second Corinthians 10:5 (AMP) says:

> *We are **destroying sophisticated arguments** and every exalted and proud thing that sets itself up against the [true] knowledge of God, and we are **taking every thought and purpose captive to the obedience of Christ**.*

We can choose to be disobedient, full of fear, and run from our God-given destinies concerning this assignment to speak the Word of the Lord to a people who no longer want to hear the truth. Or we can surrender to the will of the Father and embrace all of His plans and purposes for us for such a time as this. Mordecai's words for Esther:

> *Do not think in your heart that you will escape in the king's palace any more than all the other Jews. For if you remain completely silent at this time, relief and deliverance will arise for the Jews from another place, but you and your father's house will perish. Yet who knows whether you have come to the kingdom for such a time as this?* (Esther 4:13-14).

Persecution is coming to the Church. What form of persecution this will be only time will tell. And although we don't seek persecution, we certainly don't run and hide from it by compromising. Let's remind ourselves that even during times of persecution, God is faithful (2 Timothy 2:13) and His Word is truth (John 17:17). He is the same yesterday, today, and forever (Hebrews 13:8). He will never leave us, or forsake us (Hebrews 13:5). If God is for us, who can stand against us? (Romans 8:31).

We are all called to be evangelists who are ready in season and out of season. We have taken and hidden the Word of the Lord deep in our hearts for such a time as this. And we are willing and able by the great power of His Spirit to give a timely word that pierces the hearts of our listeners. Keeping in mind that it is not by our charismatic nature or our fancy words that we are given the responsibility to evangelize the lost with—but by the power of His might.

> ..."*Not by might nor by power, but by My Spirit,*" *says the Lord of hosts* (Zechariah 4:6).

The times and seasons for the Church worldwide has changed. We have been called outside of our meeting halls and into the thick of the battle. According to Second Timothy 4:2-5, what is our end time assignment?

- Preach the Word!
- Be ready in season and out of season.
- Convince, rebuke, and exhort with long-suffering and teaching.
- Endure afflictions.
- Do the work of an evangelist.
- Fulfill your ministry.

Let's look at each of these specific assignments in-depth.

Preach the Word!

This portion of Scripture is not just speaking to the fivefold ministry—apostles, prophets, evangelists, pastors and teachers (see Ephesians 4:11), but to all believers. And yes, in these last days we all need to be preaching the Word of God in a way that those around us can hear the message.

The apostle Paul writes to us in First Corinthians 9:19-23 (NIV):

Though I am free and belong to no one, I have made myself a slave to everyone, to win as many as possible. To the Jews I became like a Jew, to win the Jews. To those under the law I became like one under the law (though I myself am not under the law), so as to win those under the law. To those not having the law I became like one not having the law (though I am not free from God's law but am under Christ's law), so as to win those not having the law. To the weak I became weak, to win the weak. I have become all things to all people so that by all possible means I might save some. I do all this for the sake of the gospel, that I may share in its blessings.

Just what is Paul saying to us in this portion of Scripture? Are we to be hypocrites and deny our faith because someone else believes different from who we believe, or that they are in a different place spiritually? Certainly not! What Paul is sharing here is how to minister with Christian family love, one to another. I believe what he says in Philemon 1:6 makes the message clear, *"That the sharing of your faith may become effective by the acknowledgment of every good thing which is in you in Christ Jesus."*

A hellfire-and-brimstone message might be what a hardened criminal needs to hear, but it probably will not reach your next-door neighbor. It would probably be best to share from your heart with them your real-life testimonies about your personal trials and God's undeniable faithfulness to you, given with an opportunity to pray for them to receive Jesus as their Savior.

Sing to the Lord; praise his name. Each day proclaim the good news that he saves. Publish his glorious deeds among the nations. Tell everyone about the amazing things he does. Great is the Lord! He is most worthy of praise! He is to be feared above all gods (Psalm 96:2-4 NLT).

A word of caution—stay clear of the "Seeker Friendly" approach that is non-confrontational with sin, or the "Hyper-Grace" movement that slanders the Gospel message of repentance. Both movements have caused serious casualties and sent many to hell thinking that their godless lifestyles didn't matter, when in reality these lifestyles cost them their salvation.

> *Come near to God and he will come near to you. Wash your hands, you sinners, and purify your hearts, you double-minded* (James 4:8 NIV).

Be Ready In Season and Out of Season

It is vital in these last days to be ready in season and out of season to give an account to others about our faith in our Lord. We never know when an opportunity will arise and we will be face to face with someone in need of the Good News of Jesus Christ. These opportunities will continue to present themselves to all of God's people during these turbulent times.

> *But sanctify the Lord God in your hearts, and always be ready to give a defense to everyone who asks you a reason for the hope that is in you, with meekness and fear; having a good conscience, that when they defame you as evildoers, those who revile your good conduct in Christ may be ashamed* (1 Peter 3:15-16).

Monica's In Season and Out of Season Ministry Opportunities

Many of my readers are familiar with Monica's name from my other books. We have watched her grow from needing and receiving healing from two incurable eye diseases to ministering healing to those around her.

She wrote to me:

Several months ago before we started "quarantine" due to COVID-19, my pastor asked me to lead a Wednesday night Bible study. It was kind of a spur-of-the-moment thing, so I didn't have much time to prepare, but immediately the Lord said Psalm 91. I still wasn't sure exactly what I was to teach on, but the Lord made it clear that I was to teach our group that night how to apply His Word in their life. Psalm 91 came to me again. I basically used Becky's teaching straight out of her book, *Conquering the Spirit of Death,* Chapter 14, "Facing the Fear of Death in these Last Days" pages 222-225.

A man attended that night with his wife who had been back and forth to kidney doctors and they were about to put him on a transplant list. He only has one kidney as he lost the other one to cancer many years ago. At the end of the teaching I had all of those in attendance come to the front and I taught them how to speak to that kidney. His wife was there and she was taking it all in.

It was very powerful and I felt like it was right out the "Becky Dvorak playbook"!!! This man, Kevin, went back to the doc a week later and his kidney function had begun to increase. Being new to the healing message, he had a few setbacks and was a bit discouraged, but with more instruction and prayer support he is now doing much better. And this past Sunday he rededicated his life and was baptized in water again.

I am finding that I am just sharing and encouraging many on an individual level. Opportunities to minister to people come up daily, and I don't want to miss anything, ya know??!!!

Monica's ministry encompasses:

- The ministry of helps alongside her local pastor and leading Bible studies, which is also a Bible teaching ministry.
- The ministry of helps with me as an intercessor—one that lifts up in prayer author Becky Dvorak and my Healing and Miracles International.
- The ministry of reconciliation—as we should all be— and ministers in the power of His might according to the needs of the people presented to her.
- Her ministry calling that is very needed within the Body of Christ today. Perhaps, this is the calling God has for you in these last days.

Convince, Rebuke and Exhort with Long-Suffering and Teaching

During these trying times, many will fall away from the faith, but at the same time many will call upon His name as their Savior. These people need discipleship in the Way, the Truth, and the Life of Christ. God needs and wants you to make disciples in the name of the Lord with patience and teaching, bringing people to the saving knowledge of the Lord Jesus Christ.

In this discipleship process, you need to be the older and wiser big brother or sister to them and risk being misunderstood, while leading them through God's Word, teaching them right from wrong. Things may get complicated with your new disciples, they will disappoint and hurt you. Try to remember when you were in their shoes and you needed someone to take you by the hand and train you how to live a new way that was well pleasing to the Lord.

Convince

There is nothing more convincing than listening to someone who actually believes what they are saying, and puts real action behind their words.

Stephen, in the Book of Acts you read about earlier, not only believed what he was preaching to the crowd, he was willing to risk his life for Christ. It says of him in Acts 6:8, *"And Stephen, full of faith and power, did great wonders and signs among the people."* These signs and wonders have a profound effect on the listeners. You may be thinking to yourself, *Yeah, but they murdered him!*

Do you know who was present when Stephen gave up his spirit to the Lord? A powerful man named "Saul" who later had a divine encounter with Messiah Himself. This man was born again and became the mighty man of God—the apostle Paul.

Stephen and his reputation of being full of Holy Spirit, walked in signs and wonders, did not back down to his allegiance to the Lord and his faith-filled words preached even with his last breath no doubt had a profound impact on Saul.

Whether or not any of us will be martyred for our faith, only God knows. But let's live like Stephen did and be known for being full of Holy Spirit, having a good reputation, walking in signs and wonders that wow people by the power of God working in us for the glory of the Lord, being totally and uncompromisingly sold out for the Lord, and preaching the gospel of Jesus Christ even with our last breath.

Rebuke

When it comes to rebuking someone, most of us agree that it is unpleasant. Remember to rebuke the action and avoid unnecessary insults. This way, the receiver has less chance of being offended and will hear the correction you have to offer. *"For those whom the Lord loves He corrects, even as a father corrects the son in whom he delights"* (Proverbs 3:12 AMP).

Now no chastening seems to be joyful for the present, but painful; nevertheless, afterward it yields the peaceable fruit of righteousness to those who have been trained by it (Hebrews 12:11).

A brother offended is harder to win over than a fortified city, and contentions [separating families] are like the bars of a castle (Proverbs 18:19 AMP).

Although rebuking someone is not easy to do, it is a must. When we see a fellow believer doing something wrong, we need to go to that person in love and speak up. Our words of loving correction may be what sets the person on the right path again.

Exhort

To exhort someone is merely to encourage or admonish the person to do something. A word of exhortation goes a long way. The following are a few biblical examples of exhortation.

To use a real-life situation, let's consider a political example of a heated and fiery topic no matter who you are talking to. Let's say you are conversing with your neighbor about the Lord and the conversation takes a negative turn to blaming all health problems on an elected official. Instead of arguing with your neighbor, use the Word of God from Second Timothy 2:1-2 that exhorts us with these words, *"Therefore I exhort first of all that supplications, prayers, intercessions, and giving of thanks be made for all men, for kings and all who are in authority, that we may lead a quiet and peaceable life in all godliness and reverence."*

Offering to pray right there on the spot for that particular leader for wisdom from God concerning the situation can immediately defuse the contention. If the person refuses to pray, say something like, "Well, then I just need to go home right now and pray about this." And do just that—go home and pray for the individual, and for your neighbor.

Here's another example of using the Word of God to exhort someone. You are with a very negative and sickly person who only wants to tell you all their physical woes. Be a little aggressive and interject a word of exhortation from the Bible saying, "You know the Bible tells us in Proverbs 18:21, *'Death and life are in the power of the tongue, and those who love it and indulge it will eat its fruit and bear the consequences of their words.'* Let's use the power of our positive words and pray into your situation." Start to pray right then and there a prayer of faith over the person's health and healing. If the person gets all bent out of shape with you about it, gently dismiss yourself from the conversation and walk away.

If you become an exhorter instead of a discourager, you will see that when lost and hurting people have a need, they will seek you out for your exhortation and prayers of faith.

Endure Afflictions

Something that probably causes more confusion and dissension than anything else in the Body of Christ is the topic of being told we are to endure afflictions. And the culprit behind this dissension is the lie that God is the author of evil. To put the fire out of this lie, let's look at the "acts of God." Acts of God, what are they? We are accustomed to hearing newscasters declare a natural disaster as an "act of God." But is it really? Is that an accurate description?

When society no longer believes that satan exists or that hell is an actual place, it blames the Creator for destructive events. When they say that there are many roads that lead to salvation, there is confusion about who God is. And therefore, humankind makes their own gods and anyone's description of the nature and character of their god is confused and accepted as the true god, when in actuality it is a man-made god, not the One True God.

And sad to say, there are many Christians who do not study the Bible for themselves and do not know who God is or what His acts really are. So they blame the tragedies in life as God's will and turn bitter toward Him.

Is God responsible for tragedies? No. His Word tells us in John 10:10, *"The thief does not come except to steal, and to kill, and to destroy. I [Jesus] have come that they may have life, and that they may have it more abundantly."* The thief is satan and he comes to steal, kill, and destroy us, and he causes tragedies to devastate us and our loved ones. I use John 10:10 to judge any situation that is before me. If the circumstance brings any form of destruction, then I know satan is responsible. This verse helps to keep life simple, and truth also sets us free (see John 8:32).

Jesus warns us in John 16:33, *"These things I have spoken to you, that in Me you may have peace. In the world you will have tribulation; but be of good cheer, I have overcome the world."* He is forewarning us that in this fallen world we will pass through difficulties, yet we can still be cheerful. He's not making light of the situation, but revealing to us the safe place in Him where we will have peace.

In Luke 5:12-16, we read about a man who was full of the plague of leprosy. This plague was deadly and incurable. By the powers of faith, love, and compassion, Jesus cleansed the man and made him whole again.

Today, there are many plagues in this world, especially as we are nearing closer to the return of Jesus. The enemy is fighting against humankind, lurking in every corner to bring destruction; but Jesus on the other hand wills to make us whole by delivering us from plagues. Plagues are part of the curse, and Jesus delivered us from the effects of all forms of the curse by transforming into the curse for us. Galatians 3:13, *"Christ has redeemed us from the curse of the law, having become a curse for us (for it is written, 'Cursed is everyone who hangs on a tree')."*

In Luke 8:43-48, we read about a woman who had a problem that no one knew how to cure. She was bleeding for twelve years and was slowly dying. But with God all things are possible, including cures for the human body when the medical field doesn't know what to do.

First John 3:8 (AMP) tells us why Jesus came to this earth:

The one who practices sin [separating himself from God, and offending Him by acts of disobedience, indifference, or rebellion] is of the devil [and takes his inner character and moral values from him, not God]; for the devil has sinned and violated God's law from the beginning. **The Son of God appeared for this purpose, to destroy the works of the devil.**

By His blood, Jesus dissolved the power of satan and all of his evil ways over us.

Matthew 8:23-27 recalls the amazing testimony of how Jesus calms the wind and the waves. And He wills to do the same for us and through us, whether the storms are spiritual, emotional, or physical. He gives to us His authority over satan and all of his wicked works in Luke 10:19, *"Behold, I give you the authority to trample on serpents and scorpions, and over all the power of the enemy, and nothing shall by any means hurt you."* Acts of God that we can see through these verses are:

- He is a life-giver and wills to give life to us in abundance.
- He is a peace giver even during difficult times.
- He provides a safe place in Him during tribulations.
- He wills to cleanse us from modern-day plagues.
- He is able to cure the incurable.
- He dissolves the power of satan over us by the power of His blood.
- He shares His authority with us over satan and all of his wicked works.

Though the world and even some of God's people may falsely accuse God of being responsible for tragedies, sickness, disease, plagues, and deadly weather, and call these tribulations "Acts of God," we who choose to seek the truth of God's Word can see these accusations are false. In reality, He is the giver of life and gives us abundant life.

Fulfill Your Ministry

You may read this subtitle and ask yourself, *What ministry?* I'm glad you asked! In Second Corinthians 5:20 we are called, *"ambassadors for Christ."* The moment you become born again, you become an ambassador for the Lord. And yes, each one of us is commissioned to the ministry of reconciliation.

We can all agree that today's world needs healing in every area of life—spiritual, mental, emotional, and physical healing. All too often infirmities in these areas are interlinked and one area affects the other area. God is raising up the entire Body of Christ, including you, to restore broken people back to Himself.

> *So we are ambassadors for Christ, as though God were making His appeal through us; we [as Christ's representatives] plead with you on behalf of Christ to be reconciled to God* (2 Corinthians 5:20 AMP).
>
> *But all these things are from God, who reconciled us to Himself through Christ [making us acceptable to Him] and gave us the ministry of reconciliation [so that by our example we might bring others to Him]* (2 Corinthians 5:18 AMP).

Tiffany Finds and Fulfills Her Ministry Calling

Since childhood, Tiffany's desire in life was to become a doctor, because she realized she wanted to help people. Although she had been in church all her life, Tiffany actually came to know Christ as her personal Savior when she was a college student. This was when she realized she could help people in a different way.

Tiffany will never forget the night when she was introduced to Christ through the plan of salvation. Two mature ladies in the faith spent time with Tiffany, discussing the Gospel message and answering her many questions until she really understood it. She appreciated those moments and the time these ladies spent with her because it set her on a path that would change her life forever.

As a result of this intimate meeting with these sweet Christian women, Tiffany became totally on fire for God. But as a lay person, not having any titles as a pastor, minister, deaconess, or anything like this, she didn't know how she could really make an impact and influence people for the Kingdom.

The shift came on her wedding day, twenty years ago, when she married her husband, Dexter. In marrying him, she joined a lot of their other friends who married around the same time. Tiffany was shocked when only a few years later many of her friends ended up divorcing. This was very hard for her to handle, because, like Tiffany, her friends were saved, knew the love of Christ, and also loved their spouses. Because this was the case, why were so many of her Christian friends divorcing?

Instead of sitting on the sidelines just watching this happen in more Christian marriages, Tiffany felt a burning inside to help women take a deeper dive in their relationship with Christ by learning the love of Christ, understanding their identity, and hearing the voice of God so they could grow in their intimacy with Him—and ultimately their relationships with others.

Tiffany's heart is to help married women strengthen their marriages and pursue their purpose. She also helps single women prepare themselves for marriage and understand their identity. Tiffany has learned to roll up her spiritual sleeves to help women grow in their intimacy with Christ and with others. She has learned what her ministry is and continues to fulfill it for the glory of the Lord.

God wants you to understand your calling too, so He can use you to bring about the fullest extent of His glory through you while this present earth is winding down.

Tiffany's healing ministry encompasses:

- The ministry of inner healing.

- Helping restore the mind and emotions of hurting women.

- The ministry of reconciliation—restoring women into right relationship with their heavenly Father.

- Teaching them who they are in Christ, which heals the wounded spirit within them.

- Helping restore broken marriages.

This healing ministry is much needed within the Church and outside of the Church today. Perhaps, the Spirit of God is calling you to do something similar for Him.

We've discovered how God expects us to preach the truth, and to be ready in season and out of season to do so. In the next chapter we discover that the Spirit of the Lord is calling us to go into the fields of the Great Harvest. Are we willing to go and do what He desires for us?

Prayer

Dear Father God, we accept Your assignment during these last days to preach the Word to a people who no longer want to hear it. Give us the strength, courage, wisdom, and plan to preach and teach Your holy message to everyone we meet. For Your great glory we preach the Word, amen and amen.

Faith Assignment

With the message of the Lord that we are to preach the Word to people who no longer want to hear about the One True God and His saving grace, pray for wisdom daily to know what to say and to whom. Pray for divine appointments that God sets up for you this day. When people say they don't feel well, offer to pray with them for healing. If you notice that someone is depressed and discouraged with life—offer to pray for them for peace and joy. While a coworker, family member, or a friend or acquaintance mentions to you that they just don't know how to make ends meet, offer them a word of encouragement, pray for them, and give them a little something to help lighten their financial load that day. As you prove yourself faithful to God with these divine appointments, He will bring more opportunities your way to speak the truth of the Lord in love. And always offer to pray and lead them to the Lord if you are unsure about their salvation.

Questions to Ponder and Answer for Chapter 5: God Expects Us to Preach the Truth

1. What are you called to be?

_____

_____

_____

2. What do you do with the Word in these last days?

_____

_____

_____

3. How are you to be ready?

_____

_____

_____

4. According to Second Timothy 4:2-5, what should people do in these last days?

_____

_____

_____

5. There isn't anything more convincing than to do what?

_____

_____

_____

6. When it comes to rebuking someone, how should it be done?

_____

_____

_____

7. What does it mean to exhort someone?

_____

_____

_____

8. As discussed in this chapter, what causes more confusion and dissension than anything else in the Body of Christ?

_____

_____

_____

9. Is God responsible for tragedies? If not, who is responsible?

_____

_____

_____

10. It is vital in these last days to be ready in season and out of season to do what?

_____

_____

_____

11. According to 2 Corinthians 5:20 what are you?

_____

_____

_____

Personal Assessment

Am I ready and willing to share the Gospel of Jesus Christ to a lost and dying world that is in great need of the Savior? Am I willing to spend a few minutes and pray daily for the divine appointments that Holy Spirit wants to arrange for me to meet with those who are ripe for the harvest?

Group Discussion

Discuss together the message of this chapter about accepting the command of the Lord to preach the Word to a world that no longer wants to hear it. Brainstorm together ideas that you can put into action immediately to preach the uncompromised Word of God.

6

The Last Days Harvest

Word of the Lord

The Lord of the Harvest would say to you,

> The field is ripe and ready to harvest. And I am asking you to be about My business and win the people in these final days to Me. I have called and appointed you to specific people, and I have cleared the pathway to the field for you to work and bring them into the Kingdom. I have equipped you with the tools necessary to unloose them from the bondage they are in. Go forth and reap a rich harvest for My glory. I and My Father are with you, and My Spirit is working through you—let Him work through you, and they will come unto Me and be with Me for eternity. Now go and work the field.

The lost who are civil in nature, ask, "What is going on?" And you ask, "Why all the hate, violence, senseless killing, and destruction around us?" Because the world needs Jesus. Will you share Him today?

Who Will Go for the Lord?

The latter days are upon us. The enemy, satan and his demonic forces, are ramping up their efforts against the human race. The inhabitants of earth are being driven by cultural wars, innocent people are being struck down, and peaceful protests are turning into riots and looting. These events, in addition to mandatory shutdowns, are causing great oppression on the business communities. And this in turn drives up prices for the products being sold on the shelves. Families are becoming impoverished. The health and well-being of people worldwide are being stricken by plagues and pestilence, not to mention the effects this is causing on the emotional and mental health of the people. Extreme weather is releasing great destruction in its pathway.

Life has been devalued, babies are being murdered while in their mother's wombs, and many are being terminated on the birthing tables. Suicide and assisted suicides are at an all-time high. Innocent people are being sent to jail while convicted criminals are being set free; senseless shootings and killings are taking place; people are angry, full of hate, confused, and hurting. And even worse, multitudes of people are dying before they have the opportunity to fulfill their destinies, and the masses are going to hell in grievous numbers.

The enemy is not leaving one stone unturned. If he sees anything with even the slightest hint of goodness and God, he rages war against it. Why? Because he wants to steal, kill, and destroy (see John 10:10.)

Yet in the midst of all this corruption, the words of the Lord call out to the people in Isaiah 45:22, *"Look to Me, and be saved, all you ends of the earth! For I am God, and there is no other."* And while God cries out to the lost, He calls out to His people, the Church, *"The harvest truly is great, but the laborers are few; therefore pray the Lord of the harvest to send out laborers into His harvest"* (Luke 10:2).

If we don't go into this harvest field, the people can't hear the truth about the One True God who saves. And just as it asks in Romans 10:14-15, *"How then shall they call on Him in whom they have not believed? And how shall they believe in Him of whom they have not heard? And how shall they hear without a preacher? And how shall they preach unless they are sent?"*

The Spirit of the Lord is calling us the Church to rise up to the occasion in these chaotic times and accept the call in Isaiah 6:8, *"Whom shall*

I send, and who will go for Us?" Will we, the people of God respond like Prophet Isaiah did? *"Here am I! Send me."* Will we gladly be the beautiful feet who preach the gospel of peace and bring glad tidings of good things? (See Romans 10:15.)

People Are "Hangry" for the Lord

No, this is not a typo in the subheading. "Hangry" is the combination of the words *hungry* and *angry*, which is the spiritual state of people in the world today. They are spiritually hungry, but without God they are angry and feeding on things that don't fulfill their spiritual hunger. Only a right relationship with the Bread of Life, Jesus Christ, can fill, fulfill, and satisfy their spiritual hunger.

In John 6:35 Jesus says of Himself, *"I am the bread of life. He who comes to Me shall never hunger, and he who believes in Me shall never thirst."*

People serve the deceiver, satan. Oftentimes this is out of ignorance, but certainly always out of rebellion. The devil, the father of all lies, churns up people's emotions with dissatisfaction, evil, hate, strife, unforgiveness, vengeance, murderous thoughts and intentions, selfishness and confusion, and they grieve a loss that they can't begin to understand—eternal life. They feel condemned, and spiritually speaking they are. They have taken on the devil's nature and ways and are angry with God and those who profess to believe in Him.

John 8:44 speaks of their spiritual condition and the devil they serve:

> *You are of your father **the devil**, and the desires of your father you want to do. He was a murderer from the beginning, and does not stand in the truth, because there is **no truth in him**. When he speaks a lie, he speaks from his own resources, for **he is a liar** and the father of it.*

So yes, the people of the world are "hangry," and in need of the Gospel of peace, glad tidings, and the good things of the Lord that we possess. The lost have spiritual hunger pains that they don't understand, and they have an anger that won't subside unless they make peace with God. And without salvation, there is no hope for them.

The Church Carries the Hope

We have what the world needs—hope. God is calling out to His beloved, you and me, to rise up to the occasion set before us and deliver Hope—Jesus, the Deliverer, Healer, and Savior of the world.

But we can't accomplish the task in front of us if we continue to doubt our calling to be about our heavenly Father's business and present the end time harvest of lost souls to Him. We have the hope that they need. If we don't go and harvest the fields, satan will.

The world needs the Church to be stronger than ever now. The lost can't afford to be among a body that's weak in the faith. They need us to be willing and bold to express our faith with our words and actions. They are in desperate need for the perfect love of God to arise within us. They are dying for God's touch of healing from our hands.

Without understanding, the lost are warring for the peace of God within us, but don't know how to get it. They are crying out for the joy of the Lord that strengthens us on a day-to-day basis.

God designed us with the same needs that can only be met by being relational with the Father. There is a global epidemic of fatherless individuals who are bound by an orphaned spirit and in need of adoption by the heavenly Father. They are searching for a family that will accept them. Will we bring them into the family of God?

God has Called and Equipped Us with the Right Tools

God has called us to be the healers on earth and to be lovers of God. He created us to be like Himself—faith beings. We are joy producers and peacemakers in this lost world. We are the family of God that reaches out to the lost and wins them to Father God. He has equipped us with the right tools that will lead the lost to eternal salvation. He has given to us a basic method to reach the lost and hurting people as He did when He walked the earth. The supernatural realm of signs and wonders steals their attention, it calls them to the redeeming message of the Word. And one of these supernatural tools that Jesus gives to us is healing—the healing of the spirit, soul, and body. Some of the ways He works healing through us is by love, faith, joy, peace, and the spirit of adoption.

Healers on Earth—Heal

The Messiah, Jehovah Rapha, is our Great Physician. It is by the power of His atoning blood that we are healed according to Isaiah 53:4-5. In no way am I taking away from the power of His blood. In fact, my entire life and ministry is wrapped around this fact. So, I ask you to turn on your spiritual ears and hear the Word of the Lord in what I am about to say.

We are created in the mirror image of Elohim—Father, Son, and Holy Spirit (see Genesis 1:26-28.) As Jesus is, so are we on this earth (see 1 John 4:17). We are His ambassadors (see 2 Corinthians 5:20). As His ambassadors we say what He says. We do what He does. We are empowered by His Holy Spirit (see Acts 1:8). By His own words of affirmation, Jesus Christ prophesies to us who believe in Him, that we will do what He does, and greater works than these will we do in His name. Please read His words in John 14 with your own eyes:

Most assuredly, I say to you, he who believes in Me, the works that I do he will do also; and greater works than these he will do, because I go to My Father. And whatever you ask in My name, that I will do, that the Father may be glorified in the Son. If you ask anything in My name, I will do it (John 14:12-14).

As His ambassadors, we live so far below what He ever intended for us. We true believers in Christ must see ourselves clothed with His Spirit. See ourselves wearing His rich robes of righteousness (see Isaiah 61:10). And not because of anything we have done, but because of everything He has accomplished for us at Calvary.

Wherever He leads us we will go, and we will do as He would do. If someone is demon-possessed, we will command it out of them. If someone is sick, we will extend our healing hands toward them. If they are deaf, we will be quick to minister to them in faith to hear again. If they are blind, we will not hesitate to extend the power of faith for seeing eyes. Whatever the need of the person standing near us may be, we will see ourselves as the Messiah sees and declares us to be the healers on earth. And all that we do—we do in the authority of His name.

So from now on, wherever we go in the name of the Lord our Messiah, we will expect company to show up—signs and wonders that glorify our King, Jesus Christ:

These signs will accompany those who have believed: in My name they will cast out demons, they will speak in new tongues; they will pick up serpents, and if they drink anything deadly, it will not hurt them; they will lay hands on the sick, and they will get well (Mark 16:17-18 AMP).

Lovers of God—Love

Earlier in this work I stated that one of the most basic needs of all people is to be loved. And plainly put, we can't reach the people if we do not love them first. This love is more than a mutual respect for one another, it is a supernatural power from God that heals all wounds.

We are called the lovers of God (see 2 Timothy 3:4); and as His lovers, everything we say and do must come from a heart of love for Him, toward them. The only reason this love is birthed within our hearts for others can be found in First John 4:19, *"We love because He first loved us."*

This world does not know love, and without a right relationship with Him, they will never know what true love is. We who know God, know this love. Romans 5:5 (AMP) tells us, *"Such hope [in God's promises] never disappoints us, because God's love has been abundantly poured out within our hearts through the Holy Spirit who was given to us."*

Our calling as lovers of God is to share His love with those in our arena of influence. Where has God placed you? Be upright in this calling, and lead them to the knowledge of His saving grace, before it is too late for them.

This lost world has a great need for the true lovers of God to move into their rightful position and love as He loves.

Faith Beings—Live by Faith

We are created in the image of God, and He is not full of fear, but faith. And so should we be, like Him—faith beings. Faith is a solid foundation for us to stand on, and yet for many believers their foundation of faith is like sinking sand. It's time to undo a foundation of doubt and unbelief and rebuild our foundation. And we can!

Faith comes by hearing and hearing by the Word of God (Romans 10:17). An easy remedy to rebuild a weak foundation of faith is to pick up our Bibles and start reading about the mighty men and women of faith, and learn from their life lessons. Another way to rebuild our faith foundation is to pay attention to what we listen to. Television rules the homes of many Christian families. Ungodly and oftentimes mindless shows destroy our foundation of faith. The old adage, "Garbage in—garbage out!" should be written and attached to our TV and computer screens.

Another way to destroy the power of faith in our lives is to surround ourselves with people of doubt and unbelief. When we are with this type of people on a consistent basis, their lack of faith will have an effect on our lives. This fact leads us to another faith-building point—we have to choose our friends wisely (Proverbs 12:26).

We must be wise in these pressing times. Guarding the following four areas will protect us and help strengthen our foundations of faith:

1. Read our Bibles again.
2. Pay attention to what we listen to.
3. Guard what we watch on television and the Internet.
4. Choose friends of faith.

As we strengthen our own personal faith, we can then reach out with the power of faith to the faithless and believe for their miracles to manifest.

Joy Producers—Rejoice

As joy producers, we are to make a joyful noise unto the Lord (see Psalm 100:1). And being joyful is more than having fun, it's about creating happy people. Joy is a supernatural power of Holy Spirit that fills people with the strength of the Lord (see Nehemiah 8:10). We are told twice in Philippians 4:4 to rejoice in the Lord—not just sometimes, but always.

A happy Christian is a contagious one. We can learn to carry His joyous strength inside us wherever we go and share this medicine of joy with everyone we come in contact with. Joy heals the mind and the emotions and strengthens the physical body. Joy makes eternity with Christ all the more real within our hearts. Joy is a healer (see Proverbs 17:22).

This world is being crushed under a spiritual heaviness, and downtrodden souls need us to create an atmosphere of joy that will draw them to come near us. When they get close to us, they are uplifted and desire our reason for this joy—Jesus.

Be the joy makers we are created to be and make a joyful ruckus for the Lord. Release this joy and allow it to begin to heal all those who come near us today.

Peacemakers—Make and Maintain the Peace of God

The world is in turmoil and warring among themselves. The wounds of hate have been ripped open once again. These are deeply infected wounds, and the enemy has thrown salt into them making people scream out in agony. Our society is in need of peacemakers who dare to rise up and make and maintain the peace of God. Matthew 5:9 (AMP) declares, *"Blessed [spiritually calm with life-joy in God's favor] are the makers and maintainers of peace, for they will [express His character and] be called the sons of God."*

This means we have to be willing to demonstrate how to make peace when little or none exists. Part of peacemaking involves listening and sharing in love, laying down pride, learning to be humble, and preferring others before ourselves. This means discipleship, which has been a weak area in the Church that must become strong again.

There is much to learn from the Lord's example. The following is a list of six steps for us to learn and put into practice:

1. Jesus made disciples by first giving the invitation to follow Him—we must do the same. Release the evangelistic call to follow Him.
2. Jesus developed relationship with His disciples.
3. Jesus taught them the ways of the Lord.
4. Jesus showed them by His own personal example how to follow the ways of the Lord too.
5. Jesus loved them enough to allow them to hurt Him.

6. Jesus gave everything He had, Himself, to make and maintain the peace of God.

The Family of God—Adopts Others into the Family

We are the family of God, the mothers, fathers, brothers and sisters, uncles and aunts, and the nieces and nephews to whom the orphans and those with an orphan spirit seek to belong. We belong to the perfect family that everyone dreams about, if only we would demonstrate what God's family truly is about.

Jesus tells us in Mark 3:33-35 just who is His family:

> *But He answered them, saying, "Who is My mother, or My brothers?" And He looked around in a circle at those who sat about Him, and said, "Here are My mother and My brothers! For whoever does the will of God is My brother and My sister and mother."*

And what is His will? Matthew 28:19-20 reveals His will for us:

> *Go therefore and make disciples of all nations, baptizing them in the name of the Father and of the Son and of the Holy Spirit, teaching them to observe all things that I have commanded you; and lo, I am with you always, even to the end of the age.*

In order to go out and make disciples, we need to understand a few facts about people and evangelism. We've established one basic fact—everyone wants to be loved. They also want to be accepted and belong. Cults are well aware of this fact and that's how they go about their dirty business to deceive and entrap people into their wickedness.

So if satan's tribe knows how to falsely use these basic needs to reel in the hurting, how much more should we understand these basic needs of all people and love them for real. We can truly love people for who they are, accept them with their imperfections, and lead them into

God's family where they really do belong. It all sounds so easy, but we tend to complicate the matter.

As sons and daughters of God, it is time for all believers to get real with the world. Let them know who we truly are. Unashamedly reach out to everyone in our path with the irresistible love of God—the love that goes after the one left behind and shepherds them into all truth and grace of our Lord Jesus Christ. Matthew 18:12-14 (NLT) says:

> *...If a man has a hundred sheep and one of them wanders away, what will he do? Won't he leave the ninety-nine others on the hills and go out to search for the one that is lost? And if he finds it, I tell you the truth, he will rejoice over it more than over the ninety-nine that didn't wander away! In the same way, it is not my heavenly Father's will that even one of these little ones should perish.*

All too often we are too preoccupied with the need to manifest ourselves that we forget that without the grace of the Savior we are nothing, and have nothing to offer people. But when we humble ourselves before our God, and accept the truth that we live and move and have our being because of Him, our faith will become infectious and spread quickly to those around us.

We will see people as we ought to—through the eyes of the Father who sees into the deepest hurts and needs of every individual. No longer will we be concerned with what others may think about who we are with. What's important to God—the individual longing to be part of something they have never understood before—is the family of God.

Dear reader, we have our work cut out for us. It's time to head to the fields and harvest the orphans and those with an orphaned spirit, to reach out to them with the love of the Father, bring them to the eternal place of salvation, accept and adopt them into our family, disciple them, and present them to the Father.

For you did not receive the spirit of bondage again to fear, but you received the Spirit of adoption by whom we cry out, "Abba, Father" (Romans 8:15).

Healing Is an Evangelistic Tool

Never underestimate the power of healing, whether it be your healing or the healing of another in these turbulent days. Healing points to the Messiah. It proves that the God you have been professing all these years is real. It grabs the attention of the unbeliever: *"And the multitudes with one accord heeded the things spoken by Philip, hearing and seeing the miracles which he did"* (Acts 8:6). This is why the enemy fights so hard against this message. He is afraid of the fruit of salvation that is harvested through healing.

Take the limits off God about who can and who cannot be healed. Throughout all these years of ministering healing to people around the world, I stand amazed at just who receives their healing and who doesn't receive what God has for them. I have witnessed the most rebellious people on the streets receive instant healing, and they are so amazed that in the midst of all their rebellion that someone reached out in the name of Jesus and they were healed.

While ministering on the streets of Guatemala City, a young rebellious teenage boy was screaming obscenities in my husband's and my face because he hated who we represented—God. But when his freshly broken arm (broken in a gang fight earlier that day) was instantly healed, he stopped his filthiness and listened and heard us give the message of the Lord.

These amazing miracles proclaim loudly the Gospel of Jesus Christ and hail the praise of our Messiah. The hearts of the rebellious are absolutely stunned by the power of grace bestowed upon them as a dead baby in the womb of a young prostitute comes back to life, infected stab wounds are healed, kids with STD are set free from suffering within a moment of time. These miraculous healings confirm our evangelistic words about our loving and living God.

And God is just waiting for us to set our faith in motion on behalf of other people. When we do, great things happen.

How about we take this to your own neighborhood, the street where you live, and start with your next-door neighbor? When you hear that they are sick and dying from cancer, what are you going to do about it? Will you take the risk of rejection and reach out in the name of the Lord and share the love of God with them through a healing touch? Do you understand the impact you can start to have all around you in these last days? I am telling you, you have nothing to lose and everything to gain by being willing and obedient to the command in the Great Commission.

Let's read this great commission again and remind ourselves what the Lord would have us do:

> *And He said to them, "Go into all the world and preach the gospel to every creature. He who believes and is baptized will be saved; but he who does not believe will be condemned. And these signs will follow those who believe: In My name they will cast out demons; they will speak with new tongues; they will take up serpents; and if they drink anything deadly, it will by no means hurt them; they will lay hands on the sick, and they will recover"* (Mark 16:15-18).

The Great Commission answers our doubts and questions about what to do and say in these last days. Like the example I just shared about your next-door neighbor. You hear they are sick with cancer, and you aren't sure they are born again. But you are still fighting the flesh and the fear of people and possible rejection. Oh my, your mind and emotions are wrestling with your spirit, "Should I go and offer to pray for my neighbor?" "Is it God's will to use me this way?" "What if they get upset with me and tell me to buzz off?"

These words from Mark 16:15-18 are the words of our Savior, Jesus Christ Himself—it is not a great suggestion, it is the Great Commission. He says, *"Go!"* We don't need to question any longer whether God wants us to go and visit our neighbor. He says, *"Go into all the world."* The world includes our own neighborhoods.

We agree with the command of the Lord to go to our neighbor, but then we struggle with fear about what to say or what to do. Again, Jesus instructs us very clearly in this portion of Scripture. He tells us to *"preach the Gospel."* We can so easily talk ourselves out of eternal solutions by listening to spirits of fear and intimidation.

The Gospel of Jesus Christ is so simple, but yet so very powerful. John 3:16 is the perfect message for all people, everywhere: *"For God so loved the world that He gave His only begotten Son, that whoever believes in Him should not perish but have everlasting life."* This becomes the basis of our every message, the love of God for all people. And no matter what they have or haven't done, said or haven't said, God doesn't wish for anyone to go to hell. Don't meander around the bush with people, spell it out plainly to them. Most will appreciate your forthrightness.

And let me add here, it has never been about preaching with fancy words—it's about sharing words filled with faith and conviction, because without a doubt you believe what you say to others.

Jesus also explains more to us about our faith to evangelize the lost and hurting people around us. He simply states, If you believe...you, yes you, *"will lay hands on the sick, and they will recover."* There isn't anything difficult about obeying the Great Commission except for the obeying. But the more you love the Lord, the easier and quicker you will be at fulfilling the Commission. It will become natural for you to share and demonstrate the love of the Lord to all around you.

So what might you say to your next-door neighbor, Sam? "Well, hello Sam! Say I hear you're not doing so well, so I've come over to show my support. I'm a person of faith, and I believe in the power of prayer. I would be honored to pray for you right now. Is that alright with you?"

If he agrees, lay your hand on his shoulder and pray something like this, "Father God, in the name of Jesus I lift up my neighbor and friend, Sam, to You. I curse this wicked cancer inflicting pain and suffering upon his body. I curse every cancerous cell and tumor, I command them to die off in the name of Jesus and be supernaturally eliminated from his body. I speak words of faith into Sam's body and I command every cell, tissue, organ, and system in his body to be healed, recreated, strengthened, cancer-free, and cancer proof for the glory of the Lord, amen."

And then continue your conversation with Sam and ask him if he has ever prayed to ask Jesus to be his Savior. Depending how the conversation goes, lead him a simple prayer like this, and have him repeat it after you: "Father God, I confess that I am a sinner; I have said and done things I should not have. I ask You to forgive me of these wrong-doings. Jesus, I believe You died for my sins and rose again from the dead, and I ask You to be my Savior this day, in Your most holy name I pray, amen."

And then add some genuine reassurance, telling him that if he needs help with anything to let you know and you will do what you can. Then live up to that promise. Check up on him every couple of days, and if you see a need, meet it. Don't make him come begging for help. Reassure him every time you see him that you are standing in faith with him and praying daily for him.

A conversation and a prayer of faith for healing like this really is not intimidating for you to share, nor is it difficult for your neighbor to hear and receive from you. You might just be surprised at how the doors of friendship and personal ministry open up between the two of you.

You don't have to have heavy training to evangelize, you just simply be yourself and share from your heart what you already believe to be true.

Romans 15:18-19 says to us:

> *For I will not dare to speak of any of those things which*
> *Christ has not accomplished through me, in word and deed,*
> *to make the Gentiles obedient—in mighty signs and wonders,*
> *by the power of the Spirit of God, so that from Jerusalem and*
> *round about to Illyricum I have fully preached the gospel of*
> *Christ.*

If you will wield the power of signs and wonders, you can win both Jew and Gentile in greater numbers to the Lord in these latter days.

I Want to See People Healed Too

A man wrote to me with the following request, "I want to lay my hand on people and see them get healed. Can you please pray for me to get the same gift as you? I want to see people healed. I was healed once, and want to give it forward to as many people as possible!"

This is a frequent request, and my response to this man, "According to the Great Commission, if you believe, you will lay hands on the sick and they will be healed. What you need to do is fill yourself with the Word of God until you believe, and then begin to lay hands upon the sick in faith, and you will see them healed in Jesus' name."

And to others seeking the same as this man, I say to you—first of all, healing is a free gift, but that doesn't mean it's cheap. It came at a high price. Jesus gave all He had to see us healed in spirit, soul, and in the physical body as well. Second, what does it take to lay hands on the sick and see them healed? Faith. I personally cannot lay hands on you and you automatically have faith to believe for healing. It doesn't work that way. You have to choose to do what it takes to believe to lay hands upon the sick and see them healed.

Where Does Faith to Heal Come From?

Another word for faith could be trust. And this trust or faith for heal-ing comes from time spent in the Holy Scriptures, the Bible, concerning healing. *"So faith comes from hearing [what is told], and what is heard comes by the [preaching of the] message concerning Christ"* (Romans 10:17 AMP).

Read and study God's promises about how He wills to heal us. Embed these healing verses deep within your spirit.

> But [in fact] He has borne our griefs, and He has carried our sor-rows and pains; yet we [ignorantly] assumed that He was stricken, struck down by God and degraded and humiliated [by Him]. But He was wounded for our transgressions, He was crushed for our wickedness [our sin, our injustice, our wrongdoing]; the pun-ishment [required] for our well-being fell on Him, and by His stripes (wounds) *we are healed* (Isaiah 53:4-5 AMP).

Anointed by God

We need to reach a point in our faith where we actually believe God's words are true for us as they are for others. You truly are anointed by God for such a time as this. You are created in His mirror image; and because of this, you too are anointed like Him to go out and win the lost with amazing signs and wonders. And the only thing preventing this from manifesting in your life is you.

Read these words that Jesus spoke aloud from the Book of Isaiah concerning Himself while in the synagogue:

> Because He has anointed Me
> To preach the gospel to the poor;
> He has sent Me to heal the brokenhearted,
> To proclaim liberty to the captives
> And recovery of sight to the blind,

To set at liberty those who are oppressed;
To proclaim the acceptable year of the Lord (Luke 4:18-19).

Now, allow me to take you through the Scriptures and find the biblical evidence that you too are called as Jesus is to this lost and dying world to minister as He does on earth.

Let's examine Jesus' words, *"Because He has anointed Me,"* and search the Scriptures to find that you too are anointed for this task in today's world. Second Corinthians 1:21 from the Amplified Version of the Bible says, *"Now it is God who establishes and confirms us [in joint fellowship] with you in Christ, and who has anointed us [empowering us with the gifts of the Spirit]."*

This word *anointed* means to endue Christians with the gift of the Holy Spirit (Strong's G5548). And what happens when we are baptized with the baptism of the Holy Spirit? Acts 1:8 (AMP) tells us:

> But **you will receive power and ability** when the Holy Spirit comes upon you; and you will be My witnesses [**to tell people about Me**] both in Jerusalem and in all Judea, and Samaria, and even to the ends of the earth.

A quick study of the word *power* from Acts 1:8 on the blueletterbible .org website revealed: δύναμις dýnamis, doo'-nam-is; from G1410; force (literally or figuratively); specially, miraculous power (usually by implication, a miracle itself):—ability, abundance, meaning, might(-ily, -y, -y deed), (worker of) miracle(-s), power, strength, violence, mighty (wonderful) work.[1]

We can see through this simple word search that we are anointed as Jesus was anointed to minister as He does. This is good news—we need not be filled with doubt and unbelief concerning God's will for us in these last days as to whether or not we are called and anointed by God, because we are. You need another Scripture to back up this truth? *"Love has been perfected among us in this: that we may have bold-ness in the day of judgment; because as He is, so are we in this world"* (1 John 4:17).

God has a Healing Ministry for You

God has a plan and an arena of ministry where He desires you to heal in spirit, soul (mind and emotions), and in the physical body too. A ministry that He has designed and equipped you to be used for His glory in these last days. I want to encourage you with the following testimonies that come from a few of my personal intercessors.

Martha's Ministry Story

Many years ago when Martha was a wife and young mother of four children, she had been invited to join a prayer group. Martha gladly accepted the invitation as she was hungry for God. Although she had been raised in the church, she was to encounter God in a personal way that she had not known before.

Alma was the leader of this prayer group, and I personally came to know and love Alma too a few years before she graduated to her heavenly home with the love of her life—Jesus. Alma was not just a Christian, she also knew the Lord personally. It was her passion to lead women into this same personal relationship with the God Almighty. Martha was one of her early disciples, and the beauty of discipleship is that you multiply disciples with the same passions.

With Martha's great humor, she shares her beginning days as a newbie in the ministry of intercession. She recalls the days when her four children were very young and the only place she could find to be alone was in the bathroom. She says her kids would bang on the door asking, "How long are you going to be in there for?" And she would wittingly respond, "As long as it takes, dears!"

I share this funny side to her growing process in the ministry as you might think to yourself that you don't have the time or the perfect set up in your home to develop a ministry—but honestly, all it really takes is a willing heart and God will tend to the rest.

Martha had been trained well as an intercessor who was and is sold out to Jesus still to this day. And at the time of this writing she is 78 years young. She started a prayer group for women in her own home about thirty years ago. Martha started by seeking the Lord about whom He would have her invite. She came up with a list of about twenty-six women. And all but two eventually came in His timing. (This is in her beginning years, but has since then discipled many more women to tap into the presence of the Spirit of God.)

God has used Martha to empower women to become Spirit-led intercessors. What do I mean by this? After the women arrive at her home and settle in, they have a time of singing in worship together. Then they quiet down in the presence of the Lord. No one says anything, they just sit still in silence before God and allow the Spirit of the Lord to minister to each individual heart. After this quiet time before the Lord, they take turns sharing what Holy Spirit spoke to them about; out of this sharing develops a unique message that has been divinely inspired of the Lord for the entire group.

What Martha has empowered these women with has not only taught them to be Spirit-led intercessors, but has also taught them how to turn to Jehovah Rapha, our Healer, in their time of need and for the needs of others.

The goal of Martha's ministry is to teach the women she disciples to listen with their spiritual ears and hear what Holy Spirit wants to speak to them about their personal situations, and to learn to hear what Holy Spirit wants them to hear collectively. Holy Spirit has taught them how to have longevity in this in-home prayer group by learning to tolerate and forgive one another, and to respect where they are spiritually in their walk with the Lord.

I love the beauty of God's calling on all of our lives, and how one life can touch the lives of so many others.

Is God speaking to your heart to lead a similar group of this nature in the privacy of your own home?

What is Martha's ministry?

- First and foremost, Martha is a lover of God.
- She is an intercessor.
- Her calling is to create other lovers of God and intercessors.
- The heartbeat of her ministry is to empower women to enter into God's presence for themselves.
- To train women to hear and obey His voice and learn to be healed by their own faith.
- This is a mentoring or discipleship ministry.
- It is also a ministry of reconciliation—restoring right relationship between women and God.

This is a very important ministry today. And you may be called into this same type of healing ministry.

Terri's Ministry Story

Allow me to share another testimony of another one of my intercessors with you. One of the victims of the spirit of death is the vulnerable, those who can't fight the good fight of faith on their own, and such is the case in the newborn intensive care unit (NICU) ward. But Terri, a woman of faith, my friend, and one of my intercessors, stood in the gap for one of these precious and vulnerable babies with great results. Let's read and see just how she conquered this spirit of death on behalf of this little baby.

Terri writes,

> God has called me to minister in our local hospital by cuddling the babies in the NICU ward. Recently, I had two

consecutive nights scheduled. The following day an email was sent out to the volunteers for that night. I was taking my grand-daughter to an event that day and hesitated to respond. I kept checking to see if anyone had responded, but no one had. It was late afternoon when I took my granddaughter home and there was still no response, so I responded that I would go in that night.

The previous night I was given a baby who was fitfully crying. I prayed, "Oh Lord, please help me." We are not told the history of these babies, but the nurse shared she was three days old, unable to keep formula down, and they were thinking of transporting her to another hospital. This baby girl had an IV running and was mad! The nurse placed her in my arms with a pacifier, and asked if I was okay and left, and said to call if I needed help.

This precious, sweet baby screamed while arching her back. As I always do, I called on Jesus, "Please Lord, let this baby feel Your hands and Your heart. Let me get out of the way." And I prayed in my natural and in my spiritual language. Very soon the cries subsided and she relaxed with a cry coming just once in a while. I said, "Thank You, Jesus, for the peace for this baby." I held her for two and a half to three hours until it was time for me to leave. Again I prayed, "Oh Lord, let her continue to feel You."

I went in the next night and was assigned to hold that same baby. I was expecting the same situation as the previous night, but when I got to the room this precious little girl was quiet, and she had no IV. The nurse gave me a brief report and said she was even keeping her formula down. I began to cry as I was tell-ing her God had answered my prayers, and she agreed! I held a very content little baby that night as I continued to pray into her spirit.

While listening to Terri share this testimony with me, I asked her, "Terri, how would you say that the teachings from my books about our words and standing in faith helped you to conquer the spirit of death over this child?"

She responded, "Standing in faith is believing God at His word. Seeing His work is such a faith builder. To experience the power of our words which are so important is testimony in itself. Our words do make a difference and we should choose life-giving words. Renounce every morbid, and negative word spoken over these children, even your own negative thoughts."

I ask, "Terri, how do you speak to these babies when they are suffering with pain?"

She answers, "All I am allowed to do is hold the babies. I'm not told much about the babies for reasons of confidentiality. When I am holding an 'angry' baby that's arching their back, my voice doesn't change per se, as I want the babies to hear a soft, but confident voice. But I put emphasis on the words that declare life. (Gotta tell you the tears fall!) I pray positively into their spirit, taking authority in Jesus' name is what we are to do and then we are to expect Him to manifest. God is faithful."

As I continue to listen to Terri share with me her story, she says, "The nurses have been very open to me walking the unit praying before I go to my assignment. God prepares the hearts."

So I ask her, "Did you ask the nurses for permission to pray? Or did you just tell them that's what you are doing?"

And she responds, "Actually, I just told them and they didn't say no." She adds, "I am so humbled and overwhelmed with the goodness of God. I have never had prayers answered so quickly. Talk about a faith builder. Becky, you said to anoint the babies with prayer, and as I was coming home the other night, Holy Spirit said before I get to my assignment that I am to touch and pray over each doorway while I walk the unit, as I cannot go into these other rooms. He has led me every step of the way. I have never felt so blessed!"

Just like Terri, God has a special plan and a specific arena of ministry for you to go and fulfill the will of your heavenly Father in these last days.

> *He has delivered us from the power of darkness and conveyed us into the kingdom of the Son of His love, in whom we have redemption through His blood, the forgiveness of sins* (Colossians 1:13-14).

What is Terri's healing ministry?

- Her ministry calling is to the vulnerable.
- She is a voice and intercessor for them.
- By the power of faith-filled words she takes the spirit of death down.
- By the same power of faith-filled words, she releases healing into the bodies of vulnerable children.
- By the love of God within her, the healing gifts of compassion and mercy create healing inside of vulnerable children.

This ministry is very valuable and needed in today's world that no longer values the life of an innocent child, but God does. He raises up people like Terri to be the hands, feet, and voice for suffering little ones. A ministry similar to this one may be your calling as well.

Prayer to Find God's Ministry

Let's pray together to find that perfect place of ministry that the Author and Finisher of our faith has written and designed for us in this late hour.

Dear Holy Spirit, we desire to know where You want to use us in this late hour. We surrender our will to Your will. Plant us where You want us to be. We trust that You are all-knowing and You have designed us for this place, for this time, and for these people. May we be a light in this hour of darkness that shines so brightly for Your glory that it causes a heavenly rescue for the people we are called to help. In Jesus' mighty name, we pray, amen.

Get Ready to Receive the Great Harvest

We need to ready ourselves quickly for this great harvest that's already being gathered in great numbers during these last days.

The people coming into the Kingdom are not church hoppers, they are brand-new believers. Their lives are complicated and messy to say the least. Many, if not the majority, are unchurched. We need to remind ourselves that they were just rescued from the world. They're freshly caught in God's great net of love, but they've not been cleaned up yet. They may not be dressed like we are accustomed to or speak like we would want them to. They will come to us with ungodly lifestyles and habits that we cannot agree with. But the beauty that will shine forth from them is genuine. God's Word teaches us that people who have been forgiven the most, love Him the most.

We can read these most assuring words of Jesus to Simon about the sinful woman in Luke 7:47, *"Therefore I say to you, her sins, which are many, are forgiven, for she loved much. But to whom little is forgiven, the same loves little."*

These new believers are not bound by a religious spirit. They don't understand church politics, nor do they want to—they just want and need Jesus, and they want to be accepted and loved into the real family of God.

We need to be genuine in our own faith and loyal to our Lord Jesus. Our witness should bring the Bible to life, not cause new disciples to doubt their newly found faith. We need to love new believers in Christ without compromising God's standards. They need true disciples with integrity who will lead them in the truth of God's Word and in His ways.

He who walks with integrity walks securely, but he who perverts his ways will become known (Proverbs 10:9).

Having a good conscience, that when they defame you as evil-doers, those who revile your good conduct in Christ may be ashamed (1 Peter 3:16).

Likewise, exhort the young men to be sober-minded, in all things showing yourself to be a pattern of good works; in doctrine showing integrity, reverence, incorruptibility, sound speech that cannot be condemned, that one who is an opponent may be ashamed, having nothing evil to say of you (Titus 2:6-8).

New converts are not seeking religious programs or the latest in technology; and in all honesty, if we walk in the full power of the Spirit, hurting people will be drawn to what we really have to offer them— hope for a new beginning and eternal life with Christ.

Pastors, How Should You Prepare?

1. Start with prayer and ask Holy Spirit for His plan for your part in this end time harvest.

2. Pray for intercessors who not only love the Lord, but will love and support you.

3. Pray for true helpers who will help you do the things you don't know how to do.

4. Your number-one goal right now should be to win the lost.

5. To be super effective in these last days, *everyone* (not just paid staff) under you should be baptized in the

Holy Spirit. Teach them to pray in the Spirit—in tongues.

6. Your disciples should know how to effectively pray a prayer of salvation with someone.

7. Your team should also know how to lead others in the baptism of the Holy Spirit.

8. Train them to lay hands on the sick for healing.

9. And teach them how to love the lost and the new believer without compromising their own faith.

I was sharing a prophetic word along these same lines with a pastor who had invited me for a weekend healing conference. After hearing the Lord warn her to get ready for a great influx of new believers, she asked me, "Should I prepare a new believer's packet?" What a great question, and yes, we should do everything we can to help new believers. But be sure that the contents are biblically not religiously based, and are uncomplicated and pertinent for these last days.

New Believers' Packet

What are some topics you should include in a packet, discipleship group, online session, pdf file, or whatever platform you are using to reach out to new believers? The following are eight I suggest:

1. With all sincerity, welcome them to the family of God.

2. Explain what it means to be adopted into the family of God and the eternal security they now have in Him.

3. Teach them about the baptism of the Holy Spirit, and teach them to pray in tongues.

4. Teach them how to hear the voice of God and how to be led of His Spirit.

5. Teach them how to pray and develop a personal relationship with Jesus.

6. Assure them that their sins are forgiven.

7. Make sure they know how to grow in faith though daily time spent in His Word and in prayer.

8. Let them know how much God loves them and wills that they are healed from sickness and disease.

Prayer

Dear Father God, we repent for our unbelief in our daily part to play in the Great Commission. May we take this commission as it is meant to be, a commandment to go and do as You did and still do throughout the entire earth—to win people to You through supernatural gifts, including healing, that You have given to us. May our faith not wane when You say we are like You. In Jesus' name, amen.

A lot of thought and preparation has been laid as the foundation for our part in the last days harvest, and in the next chapter we learn how to revive and come alive once again for His glory and the advancement of His Kingdom.

Faith Assignment

This week go out into the community or workplace and share your faith with at least three people who have either been closed to your message before, or three people with whom you have never shared your faith. And allow God to use you in any of the ways shared in this chapter: a healer on this earth, a lover of God, a faith being, a joy producer, a peacemaker, or as a member of the family of God.

Questions to Ponder and Answer for Chapter 6: The Last Days Harvest

1. What does the enemy do when he sees the slightest hint of good-ness and God?

_____

_____

_____

2. Why does he rage war against it?

_____

_____

_____

3. In Luke 10:2 what does Jesus say about the harvest?

_____

_____

_____

4. What does "people are 'hangry' for the Lord" mean?

_____

_____

_____

5. What do you have that the world needs?

_____

_____

_____

6. What can't the world afford?

    _____

    _____

    _____

7. As a lover of God, everything you say and do must what?

    _____

    _____

    _____

8. What is one way that the Messiah sees and declares you to be on this earth?

    _____

    _____

    _____

9. What company can you expect to show up as you go in the name of the Lord?

    _____

    _____

    _____

10. What four areas help to guard and strengthen your faith?

    _____

    _____

    _____

11. What type of tool is healing?

_____

_____

_____

12. Can I pray for you and you have faith for healing?

_____

_____

_____

13. How is faith developed?

_____

_____

_____

14. You are anointed, like Him, to go and do what?

_____

_____

_____

15. The people coming into the Kingdom are not church-hoppers but what?

_____

_____

_____

16. Many, if not the majority, of new converts are what?

_____

_____

_____

17. New believers are not bound by what type of spirit?

_____

_____

_____

18. They don't understand church politics, nor do they want to—they just want and need who?

_____

_____

_____

19. What do they want and need?

_____

_____

_____

20. What is the first thing pastors and leaders should do to prepare?

_____

_____

_____

Personal Assessment

As I have read and studied this chapter, "The Last Days Harvest," am I being about my heavenly Father's business and winning people to the Lord? Do I see and accept that I am called to be a healer? Am I willing to release His healing power to those around me? As a lover of God, am

I honestly sharing His love with others? Knowing that I am created as a faith being, do I need to increase my level of faith for these last days? As a joy producer, do I rejoice? As a peacemaker, do I make and maintain the peace of God around me? As a member of the family of God, do I care about the lost? Do I make an honest effort to win people to Christ? In what areas do I need to make improvements to be more effective in these last days?

Group Discussion

Together with your group, be honest, and get creative and discuss immediate changes that we can implement to be more effective in bringing in the harvest of lost souls in our neighborhoods, and workplaces.

Note

1. *Blue Letter Bible* "dynamis"; https://www.blueletterbible.org/lang/lexicon/lexicon.cfm?Strongs=G1411&t=NKJV, accessed April 25, 2020.

7

Revive and Come Alive Again

Word of the Lord

The Spirit of the Lord would say to you this day,

> Revive and come alive again. Know that I am with you, My friend. Lean upon Me and I will strengthen you with the Spirit's power for this hour. I know that this fight is not light. But I give you My rights, and by My might you will overcome this fight. So do not allow your heart to take flight, but hang tight, and keep your sight on heaven's delight. The Spirit of the Lord calls out to you, "Revive and come alive again."

Where Are You Spiritually in These Last Days?

During these last days we need to carefully examine our hearts and determine where we are spiritually.

In Genesis 3, Adam and Eve sin against God and run and hide behind the bushes. The Lord comes down to the Garden to fellowship with them, but they are not where they should be. God asks Adam a very important question. He calls out, *"Adam, where are you?"*

The Lord is omniscient, He knows all things. He is not asking Adam for his physical location, but for him to identify where he is spiritually. As the time of Christ's return draws near, the Spirit of God is asking the same question, "Where are you spiritually?"

With the guidance of *"the Spirit of truth, whom the world cannot receive, because it neither sees Him nor knows Him; but you know Him, for He dwells with you and will be in you"* (John 14:17), allow His truth to guide and correct us, to save us from ourselves and the spiritual errors we have committed—before it is too late. Let's judge ourselves so Father God does not need to according to the message found in Revelation 2–4, in the letters to the seven churches.

Do You Still Love Your Savior?

We first examine the believers in the church in Ephesus and the condition of their spiritual hearts. God recognizes their deeds, their labor, their perseverance, their intolerance for evil people, and their discernment to judge false apostles. It appears with these qualities they will pass, but they don't. In fact, they fail and receive a warning to repent or they will lose their position to shine their light. Why do they fail? Because they lose their love for Christ.

Ask yourself, "Do I still love Jesus like I once did before? Do I have wandering eyes? Am I being drawn into the ways of the world due to my own sinful lust? Am I taking my Lord for granted? Is He taking second place in my life? Has He become an afterthought? Or have I fallen so out of love with Him that I give Him no thought at all?"

Pretty tough questions I have to admit. But considering where we are in the scheme of things, we need to confront these issues head-on. And if this is where we find ourselves today, we need to admit it to ourselves and to God, and repent before it is too late.

Pray this prayer of repentance if you have made Jesus second place in your life, or pray the prayer to rededicate your life to Him:

Gracious Messiah, I come humbly before You and admit with great sorrow that I have allowed You to become second place in my heart. I have allowed my spiritual eyes to wander and lust after the ways of the world. Forgive me for taking Your love for

*granted and for trampling on Your most holy grace toward me.
I have fallen, and for this I repent. Holy Spirit, show me how
to redeem the time I've lost. I recognize the signs of the season.
And by Your strength I can become all that You have called me
to be and reap this most bountiful harvest for Your glory. With
humility and a grateful heart I thank You for Your forgiveness
and grace. I declare my love and allegiance to You once again in
my life. In Your most holy name, I pray, amen.*

Do We Have Faith to Endure Persecution?

The second part of this examination applies to the church in Smyrna.
They do not hear a rebuke, only words of encouragement. Who are
they? They are the persecuted Church. He encourages them not to fear
their imminent sufferings, but to be faithful to the end.

Therefore, questions to ask ourselves are, "Do we have the level of
faithfulness it takes to endure persecution? Do we love our Lord enough
to endure whatever type of persecution may come our way?"

Let's pray this prayer of faith to endure any level of persecution in
our lives:

*Abba Father, we love You. We count it a privilege to endure any
and all persecutions for Your name in these latter days. If we
are hated, insulted, lose rights and privileges, suffer beatings,
imprisonments, even the loss of our life—we count it all joy.
And we are confident that You will never leave us or forsake us.
You are faithful and true to us, and we choose to follow You—
wherever this life may lead us. We live for Your glory, amen.*

Is God Threatening to Make War Against You?

The third part of this self-examination exposes twice in Revelation 2:13
the spiritual location of the church in Pergamum. Their dwelling is
with satan. They are a cult. Their sins are idol worship, false gods, false

teachings, and acts of immorality. They are spiritually lost and receive the warning to repent or God will make war against them.

Ask yourself, "Does my place of worship lift up Jesus as the One True God? Does it encourage idol worship? Has the message changed from sound biblical doctrine to cater to society? Is sexual immorality promoted? Am I an enemy of God?" If you can answer yes, to even one of these questions—get out of that fellowship at once! Repent and rededicate your life to your Savior and Lord.

Pray this prayer of repentance in faith—now:

Father God, I ask for Your forgiveness for my involvement in this godless and satanic fellowship. With my words and actions of faith, I decree a separation between them and me. Jesus, cleanse me from all unrighteousness, and make me whole. By the power of Your blood, I pray in faith, amen.

Are You Being Controlled by Jezebel?

The fourth section of this spiritual test is written to the church in Thyatira—the portion of God's people who refuse to repent of their worldly ways. They are so deceived that they even allow a spirit of Jezebel to lead them. Because they tolerate Jezebel, they suffer with sickness, great tribulations and difficulties, and even their children are affected with pestilence.

As a healing minister, I have never seen God's people as sick as I see them now. I believe this is a direct consequence of allowing the evils of Jezebel to reign within the Body of Christ. Ask yourself, "Am I struggling to repent from ungodliness? Am I being controlled by a person possessed with a Jezebel spirit? Am I the controlling leader in the bunch?"

Pray this prayer of repentance and salvation:

Dearest Messiah and Savior Yeshua, I repent of all sin in my life. I repent from the sin of controlling others around me. I ask for Your forgiveness. I believe in my heart that You are the Savior of the world, and that You died for my sins and rose again from the dead. I surrender my life to You this day. Yeshua, I ask You to be the Lord of my life starting this day and forever. In Your most precious name, I pray, amen.

Are You Bound by a Religious Spirit?

The fifth part of this all-important test is written to the church in Sardis, who is religious, but spiritually dead. The church receives the warning to wake up, repent, and get right with God. If she does not, God will come to her like a thief in the night.

Ask yourself, "Have I asked Jesus to forgive me of my sins and to be my Savior and Lord, or am I just going through the religious motions?" The worst words we could ever possibly hear from our Messiah are, *"Depart from Me, I never knew you"* (see Matthew 7:23). These tragic words are reserved for the "religious." The Lord desires relationship with us, not empty, meaningless religion. Let's pray in faith for salvation today.

Pray this prayer of repentance for being bound to a religious spirit:

Father God, I confess that I have been bound to a spirit of religion. I thought I was doing right, but I find now that I am lost. I have no personal relationship with You. I ask You, sweet Jesus, to forgive me of my sins, to come into my life and be my Savior and Lord. In Your holy name, I pray, amen.

Are You Faithful to God?

The sixth part of this examination addresses the church in Philadelphia. This is the second of the seven churches that does not receive a rebuke, only an admonishment with a promise. Because of her faithfulness to

God and His Word, this church will be kept from the hour of testing that will come upon the whole world.

Ask yourself, "Am I faithful to God and His Word?" If so, you are in right standing with God Himself and there is great favor over you. Are you accessing this blessed favor in these trying times that are upon us? Let's pray in faith.

Pray this prayer of faith to activate God's favor over your life:

Father God, I am blessed beyond measure to have You as my Father. I access Your divine favor over my life by the power of the redemptive blood of the Lamb of God. And because of His great sacrifice for me, I can walk in supernatural favor this day and forever. I give You great praise and honor that this favor has been bestowed upon me and my brothers and sisters in Yeshua. For Your great glory, I am thankful, amen.

Have You Lost Your Zeal for the Lord?

The seventh and final part of this exam is written to the church in Laodicea—a lukewarm church. She has no passion for the things of God, has succumbed to the riches of this world, and does not see how poor and wretched she really is. God sends His message to be zealous and repent and to obtain the true riches that money can't buy—redemption in Jesus Christ.

Ask yourself, "Am I passionate or passive for Jesus? Am I the flavorful or flavorless salt of this earth? Do I enhance the Kingdom or do I take away from it? Does my life bless You and others? Or have I lost my zeal for You?"

Pray this prayer of repentance for being lukewarm toward your Lord:

Dear Abba Father, I don't enjoy having to admit that I have become lukewarm toward You. Forgive me for being passive toward You. I didn't realize how far I have fallen; but the important thing is that I do see it now. I know I must repent, and I do repent, and sincerely want to get back my passion for You. Thank You for Your forgiveness this day, I pray, amen.

Reading through these seven mini-tests, I believe we can identify where we are spiritually today. The good news is, if we don't like where we are, we can repent and rededicate our lives to Christ, and move forward in the power of His grace this day.

Revival Is a Matter of the Heart

There's much talk for the need of revival throughout the world, our nation, and in the Body of Messiah. This is certainly true, but I'm not sure if God's people understand how to make this happen.

We can fill large auditoriums with God's people and have the most popular preachers and Christian singers. We can sing and dance throughout the night, and still not have revival. We can travel the world and revisit where amazing moves of the Holy Spirit took place, and still not enter into true revival.

Why?

Because revival is not about living off the backs of past spiritual greats. It's about what we, personally, do now. It's about the condition of our individual spiritual heart. It involves self-judgment and repentance that we studied in Chapter 3, "Plunge into the Deep Waters of Repentance." True spiritual revival resurrects deadbeat Christians and gives them a mighty dose of spiritual oxygen so that the spirit can breathe again spiritually.

True revival is not staged and doesn't come cheap. Although the fruit of it is contagious, it does not transfer from one person to another—you have to go after it for yourself. You must look at yourself with your spiritual eyes wide open and recognize your utter desperation for the Spirit of the Living God. Become the deer that David describes in Psalm

42 that is so thirsty that it pants in desperation for the water. This is how we are to desire our Lord, Jesus Christ.

As the deer pants for the water brooks, so pants my soul for You, O God. My soul thirsts for God, for the living God. When shall I come and appear before God? My tears have been my food day and night, while they continually say to me, "Where is your God?" (Psalm 42:1-3)

I grew up in Northern Minnesota in the country. The landscape was filled with trees, lakes and rivers, and lots of wildlife. It was common to see deer—many deer. My dad, brothers, uncles, and friends hunted deer. And they weren't the only ones, wolves did too. I heard many hunting stories and tidbits of advice like not letting the deer escape to the river.

So imagine being a deer that's being hunted, whether by people or wolves. Can we have an appreciation of the importance of that river to the deer? Are we able to align ourselves with a deer being hunted by enemies? No matter what we have to go through, we will not stop until we plunge into and immerse ourselves completely in the redemptive powers of the River of God and drink of His living and eternal waters.

Let me ask you, "How hungry and thirsty are you for God? Have you reached the place in your walk that you recognize He is your Source, and that your survival literally depends upon Him?"

I believe these hard times we have been going through are causing us to be thirsty again for God. And we will not be satisfied until we jump into His river all the way—totally submerged in the holy presence of our God. Nothing less will satisfy us—the true Church.

I have a testimony about Marcos, our youngest, adopted, miracle son we raised from the dead—faith manifested a series of creative miracles to bring Him back to life. I have shared his testimony all around the world, and I know it has mightily blessed many. There is so much more to his story that I want to impart what will drive home this point of being thirsty for God.

We had to fight a demon of death that was after Marcos' life ever since he was in his birth mother's womb. He came into our lives at one month of age and the spirit of death launched another deadly attack against him—sudden infant death syndrome.[1]

There is so much to his testimony that has never been told, but the following is painfully important to share:

> After he had been raised from the dead, and received a series of recreated organs by faith, he had been moved to intermediate care. A whole new set of medical staff was involved. These people were unloving and uncaring toward their patients and their families. We never met the doctors, and were not allowed to speak with the nurses and were not given any medical updates.
>
> The morning after being moved from the ICU ward, I was given a bottle with one to two ounces of baby formula to feed him. I gladly fed him his bottle. I'll never forget this moment with Marcos. With his tiny little hands he clung to that bottle and my hand as if his life depended upon that bottle and the hand that held that bottle—and in reality it did.
>
> We were in another fight against the spirit of death for his life, and this time it was starvation. I can barely even find the words to write about the world's cruelty. But it is the best example I can give to you to bring this very important spiritual lesson home to you.
>
> Again, with Marcos' tiny hands gripped tightly around that bottle and my hand, he gulped that milk down so quickly. And during the entire time he was directly looking into my eyes as his source. It was a God-moment in life, as I have

never witnessed such a young baby focus so intently into the eyes of another. I'm telling you, he was not going to let go of that bottle or my hand holding that bottle. He wanted and needed more. He was starving for nutrition, but possessed the will to live.

I have raised many babies, and I know a hungry baby when I see one. And Marcos was beyond hungry. I quickly went to the nurses' station and to my shock I was met with a threat for having the nerve (I thought common sense) to request more formula for him. I begged them for more formula for our son. And being familiar with the impoverished system of that place, I offered to give extra money to the administration's office for more formula, but was sternly warned that if I did anything I would never see my son again! I also know the corruption of that nation and I knew they meant what they said.

I contacted my husband, and we found his original doctor from the ICU ward, and he had authority and pulled a few major strings and got him released earlier than he should have been, but he knew what we were fighting against. And he made us promise him that we would take care of our son. We did.

But my point in sharing this part of the story with you is this. Marcos was starving. His little body was down to four pounds, we could see every bone in his skull, and he did not want to let go of that bottle or my hand. He squeezed tightly onto the source. He looked me straight in the eyes and would not take his eyes off of mine. This moment is truly engrained into my memory.

And I ask you, "How hungry, how thirsty are you for God?" Do you see the Redeemer not only as your Source, but *The Source?* Are your eyes fixed on Him? Are you holding on to Him for dear life? And do you possess the will to live?

Back in my introduction of this work, I mentioned the fact that what creates great miracles in the natural is birthed deep in the supernatural realm. I made it perfectly clear, "It's not me, or another human being you want to touch—that's idolatry. It's the heart of our God that you need to grab on to and not let go."

I prophesy the Messiah's words recorded in Mark 4:9 (NIV) over you, *"Whoever has ears to hear, let them hear!"*

Are you hungry and thirsty for God? Why or why not?

A Prophetic Word of the Lord

I, the Lord would say to you,

> Revive and come alive again. The moment you believed in your heart, and confessed Me as your Lord, I breathed into your spirit My breath. And you became alive, born again. But since then, you have allowed the cares of this world to darken your view. And the things you confessed that you once believed, you don't anymore. My Spirit is calling out your name and wooing you to revive and come alive again. All it takes is a simple but heartfelt cry of repentance and the dryness of your spirit will be hydrated and refreshed again.
>
> I am very near to you, I have never walked away from you. I have been longing for you to return to Me. For I love you with an everlasting love. I am for you, never against you. My Spirit is interceding for you to revive and come alive again. Return to your first love. Forget not the day you were born from above, as you entered into the presence of My great love and the newness you experienced as I washed your sins away. How My joy overflowed within you as the heaviness of this

world left you. Forsake the ways of this world, and revive and come alive again.

Allow Me to exchange My beauty for your ashes.

Give to Me all your disappointments and hurts—all that pain and suffering I bore upon My body is so you could be free from it. Lay it all down at My feet, and leave it there once and for all. Let My healing virtue flow through you. Revive and come alive again. My joy is your strength. I gave you the medicinal benefits of laughter. Learn to smile and laugh again. Enjoy the simple, but all-important things in life that really do matter. Allow My joy to revive you, and come alive again.

Your mind has been wandering in the wilderness, and temptations have been overtaking you. The way to overcome is to submit to Me and My ways. Return to My Word, and your thoughts will be renewed and victory over sin you will have. Meditate in My Word, revive and come alive again.

The days are short, and soon you will hear that mighty trumpet blow. We will meet together in the air, and what a glorious day that will be. But until then, now is the time to revive and come alive again.

The Baptism of Holy Spirit Revives Our Spirits

The baptism of Holy Spirit revives our spirit. This baptism, with the evidence of praying and speaking in tongues, is the fourth wave that is sweeping the world once again. I have never seen so many of God's people packed at the altar at all meetings to receive this special gift from the Father.

Luke 11:11-13 records the intentions of the Father:

If a son asks for bread from any father among you, will he give him a stone? Or if he asks for a fish, will he give him a serpent instead of a fish? Or if he asks for an egg, will he offer him a scorpion? If you then, being evil, know how to give good gifts to your children, how much more will your heavenly Father give the Holy Spirit to those who ask Him!

We are so blessed to have Holy Spirit in our lives. Jesus says this about Him in John 16:7 (AMP):

But I tell you the truth, it is to your advantage that I go away; for if I do not go away, the Helper (Comforter, Advocate, Intercessor—Counselor, Strengthener, Standby) will not come to you; but if I go, I will send Him (the Holy Spirit) to you [to be in close fellowship with you].

This is such an amazing description of who Holy Spirit is and what He does for us. He is our Comforter. In these very disturbing times, who doesn't need to be comforted? And we, who are born from above, have this Comforter living inside us. The Messiah goes on to say that Holy Spirit is our Advocate. We are living in an age when a lying tongue is the norm and Christians are being falsely accused left and right. But having Holy Spirit as our Advocate means He will fight for us.

Romans 8:31 (NIV) asks us the following question to build up our confidence, *"If God is for us, who can be against us?"* We know God is for us and Holy Spirit is our Intercessor. What peace fills our soul (mind and emotions) knowing that the Spirit of God is praying red-hot prayers to the Father on our behalf!

Have you ever been between a rock and a hard place and needed some advice? Holy Spirit is your Counselor and will give it to you straight. He knows all things and will guide you correctly and show you what to do in every situation. What a blessing Holy Spirit is! How about those times when you feel like you just can't keep going on? You feel depleted spiritually, emotionally, mentally, and physically. What can you do? Call out to Holy Spirit, your Strengthener, and rely upon His strength to carry you through each battle. During your greatest times of need, He is your faithful Standby. He remains your loyal support.

Holy Spirit convicts the world of their sinful ways. John 16:8 (AMP) says, *"And He, when He comes, will convict the world about [the guilt of] sin [and the need for a Savior], and about righteousness, and about judgment."*

The Word of the Lord in Isaiah 7:48 informs us that *"the Most High does not dwell in temples made with hands."* So where does He live? First Corinthians 3:16 asks us a direct question, and gives us the answer at the same time: *"Do you not know that you are the temple of God and that the Spirit of God dwells in you?"* The Spirit of God lives within every born-again believer and is waiting for you to release His resurrection power to all those around you. (See Romans 6:10-11.)

The cure for a religious spirit is the baptism of Holy Spirit. It refreshes the dried-up spirit by giving it a deep drink of Living Water. In John 7:38-39 (AMP) Jesus paints it this way for us:

> He who believes in Me [who adheres to, trusts in, and relies on Me], as the Scripture has said, "From his innermost being will flow continually rivers of living water." But **He was speaking of the [Holy] Spirit**, whom those who believed in Him [as Savior] were to receive afterward. The Spirit had not yet been given, because Jesus was not yet glorified (raised to honor).

This wave of Holy Spirit power is making its way down the highways and byways of life and strengthening persecuted saints around the world. For too long, many have been asked to walk down this painful and lonely pathway alone. And the lie given to them by the religious state of mind is if you don't endure in your own strength, you are not worthy. This is false teaching. Checking in with the Spirit of Truth, no one is worthy in their own strength. The atonement of Christ makes us worthy to God. Colossians 1:12 says, *"Giving thanks to the Father who has qualified us to be partakers of the inheritance of the saints in the light."*

Persecution has been on the increase again throughout the world, and it too is a wave that has hit the Western shores. But we are encouraged by the Lord of hosts in Zechariah 4:6, *"...Not by might nor by power, but by My Spirit."* How long have we watched our brothers and sisters around the world endure persecution? Too long. This spirit of persecution is more than mere name-calling and hurling insults at Christians, it is enforcing compromise upon the children of God—including cruelty and death if necessary. For too long, a religious spirit has held the persecuted Church in its chains of bondage. Second Corinthians 3:17 (AMP) shares a beautiful freedom promise for the Saints of God, *"Now the Lord is the Spirit, and where the Spirit of the Lord is, there is liberty [emancipation from bondage, true freedom]."*

The power of negative emotions such as depression will lift off of us when we speak in tongues, especially when we make a regular habit of activating this supernatural gift on a daily basis. First Corinthians 14:4 (AMP) speaks of a benefit of edification when we speak in tongues, *"One who speaks in a tongue edifies himself; but one who prophesies edifies the church [promotes growth in spiritual wisdom, devotion, holiness, and joy]."*

Holy Spirit is our Teacher and brings clarity to the Word for us. John 14:26 tells us that Holy Spirit is our Helper, that He will teach us all things, and even bring to our remembrance all things that Jesus said. This is great news! What if all of our Bibles were confiscated from us? Have we done as we have been taught and actually hidden the Word of God in our hearts? (See Psalm 119:11.) If we have, Holy Spirit will bring to our remembrance God's precious Word to us.

We need the help of Holy Spirit to empower us in this hour to reap this end time harvest of newly born believers. And the baptism of Holy Spirit gives exactly what we need—power. Acts 1:8 (AMP) confirms this spiritual fact for us:

> *But you will receive power and ability when the Holy Spirit comes upon you; and you will be My witnesses [to tell people about Me] both in Jerusalem and in all Judea, and Samaria, and even to the ends of the earth.*

So much is happening all around us; volatile events are occurring one upon another and sometimes it is difficult to keep up with it all in prayer. And honestly, there are times when I don't even know how to pray effectively; but I know the One who always knows the who, what, when, where, and why about every situation. So I surrender my tongue to His, and He always prays according to the Word of God.

Paul teaches us in Romans 8:26-27 (AMP):

> *In the same way the Spirit [comes to us and] helps us in our weakness. We do not know what prayer to offer or how to offer it as we should, but the Spirit Himself [knows our need and at the right time] intercedes on our behalf with sighs and groanings too deep for words. And He who searches the hearts knows what the mind of the Spirit is, because the Spirit intercedes [before God] on behalf of God's people in accordance with God's will.*

Knowing that Holy Spirit is our Helper, Comforter, Advocate, Intercessor, Strengthener, and Standby, why wouldn't we, in these last days, want to be empowered with His resurrection power that raised Christ from the dead? What are we waiting for? Step into this amazing tsunami wave of healing glory and allow His power to saturate you right now!

Question for reflection: "Am I aligned properly with Holy Spirit?" Yes or No?

Pray for the Baptism of Holy Spirit:

Dear heavenly Father, I pray and ask You right now for the baptism of Holy Spirit with the evidence of praying in tongues. I am born again. I believe that Jesus came to this earth through a virgin birth, walked this earth for thirty-three years, bled and died for my sins, and three days later rose again from the dead. I truly believe. I boldly ask You for this empowerment of the Spirit of God. Holy Spirit, come and fill me with Your power, I pray, amen.

Okay, you prayed in faith believing, now activate your faith. Open your mouth and begin to pray in tongues. Give all your fears and worries over to Him and allow His heavenly language to come forth. No praising Jesus right now, just open your mouth and allow this supernatural language to come forth.

And I add, "Holy Spirit, come down upon this reader with holy fire. Intoxicate your child with the power of Your new wine!"

Revival

Revival starts in the heart of an individual who chooses to repent and break free from the sin of mediocre Christianity. Not only do we repent of a life of haphazard faith, but we can do something about it. To revive our spiritual life, read and study the Bible with fresh purpose. Press into the power of Holy Spirit and begin with a steady flow of prayer in the Spirit—tongues. Restore our mind and emotions to the training of Holy Spirit and His ways. And not only can we read, study, and learn of the Spirit's ways, but we can put real action behind the teachings of the Bible.

Be willing to do whatever it takes to develop an intimate relationship with the Living God, and mediocre Christianity transforms into a fiery lifestyle of outrageous faith. The kind of faith where you take the limits off of God and allow Him to be Him in your daily life. Your fire for God becomes noticeable and desirable to those around you and opportunities to share your faith in the ever-loving Messiah will open up everywhere you go.

Again, true revival begins in the heart of an individual, like yourself, who is done with just going through the mindless motions of Christianity. By the power of repentance, you can move forward into real relationship with God the Father, Savior Jesus, and Holy Spirit.

The more we press into relationship with God, the more we begin to hunger and thirst for authentic fellowship. We will spot and bypass the counterfeit immediately as we enter into a meeting, and we will press for the real presence of Him. You will come to the place in your walk where you recognize His voice and break out into deep conversation anytime. You are prepared to have a divine encounter at any moment. Your communication back and forth with Him becomes so natural.

The more time we spend in studying the Bible, God's Word, and in prayer and worship, the more we become very aware of His presence around us. This is a taste of personal revival, and how it begins within us.

Four Steps to Personal Fellowship with the Spirit of God

True and personal fellowship with God the Father, our Savior Jesus Christ, and the Comforter, Holy Spirit is so important to have, especially today. It is one thing to believe God created the heavens and the earth and receive Jesus Christ as our Savior, and yes it's this initial step of salvation where we become a member of His family and a citizen of Heaven—but there is more to be had than redemption from sin and the consequences of sin. We are called into fellowship, not just a casual, fair-weather, friendly association, but deep and personal fellowship with the Trinity. The depth that the Spirit is wooing us into is a step that many have failed to take. But nonetheless, God calls us to enter into true fellowship with Him where we actually get to know Him personally. In this personal fellowship with Him is where all promises of God are supernaturally activated.

Adam and Eve had perfect fellowship with God. They communed with Him every day, and actually had a set time to meet with Him daily—in the cool of the day. And because of this fellowship they had no lack, everything was instantly provided for them. But they carelessly forfeited it all, so Jesus had to come to earth to restore what they had foolishly tossed away.

Part of what Jesus came to restore was the personal fellowship between God and people. The more we seek Him, the more we know Him; and the more we know Him, the easier it is for us to trust in His faithfulness toward us. In this strong bond of trust we can believe Him in all areas of life, including death and protection from premature death.

If a stranger came to our front door and offered to take care of our needs, we more than likely would not believe him. It's the same with the Lord, how can we trust in His promises to care for us if we don't know Him well? And if there was ever a time that we need to be able to trust Him to overcome the spirit of fear and death over our nations, the time is now. But it's difficult when we have not activated our relationship with Him.

> **God is faithful** [*He is reliable, trustworthy and ever true to His promise—He can be depended on*], *and through Him* **you were called into fellowship with His Son, Jesus** *Christ our Lord* (1 Corinthians 1:9 AMP).

According to this Scripture, God is faithful, reliable, trustworthy, ever true to His promise, and dependable. And we are called by God into fellowship with His Son, Jesus Christ. Let your heart meditate on this list of credentials for a while. Whew! No one, and I mean no one can even come close to compare to our God. We are all in need of direct fellowship with the One who has superior strength in the midst of such a problematic world.

Let's pray about our strained relationship with our Messiah God:

Messiah God, I must confess that I don't know You like I should. I ask for forgiveness as I have been born again for many years, and yet I sense in my spirit that something is lacking in my relationship with You. I now realize that I have not sought Your fellowship like You desire me to. Holy Spirit, lead me into a deeper relationship. Show me how to fellowship with You throughout my daily activities. Teach me how to sit still and be alone with You to listen to You speak to my heart, in Yeshua's name I pray, amen.

Now, take and activate what you just prayed and spend time alone with God daily.

1. Open up with a word or song of praise and worship to the Lord.
2. Spend time with Him in the Bible.
3. Talk to God; share with Him what's on your heart.
4. And then sit still, be quiet before Him, and let Him speak to your spirit.

The more you do this, the more you will know Him, and the easier it will be to trust Him as you should.

The Upper Room Experience

We all need an "upper room experience" (see Acts 2) to help nurture and strengthen our spiritual walk. To pray, worship, and fellowship with other believers in unity is truly beautiful. And this is a major part of what the family of God does together.

We should also remember that the upper room is where the Lord Jesus broke bread with His disciples the night He was betrayed. It is also the special place where the early Church was born—Pentecost. They were filled with the baptism of Holy Spirit and spoke in other tongues together.

There are two forms of power activated in this room: the power of unity and the power of Holy Spirit. These two powers operating together in our lives have the potential to bring forth great revival for God's glory. We need both these powers operating at the same time during this great harvest in the days ahead of us.

> *I appeal to you, brothers and sisters, in the name of our Lord Jesus Christ, that all of you agree with one another in what you say and that there be no divisions among you, but that you be perfectly united in mind and thought* (1 Corinthians 1:10 NIV).

> *How good and pleasant it is when God's people live together in unity!* (Psalm 133:1 NIV)

Do I pray regularly with other believers? If not, why not?

Personal Prayer Closet

As exciting as the upper room experience may be, it is also of great importance that we do not forget our personal and private prayer closets. This is the place where intimate relationship is created with our Lord.

> *And when you pray, you shall not be like the hypocrites. For they love to pray standing in the synagogues and on the corners of the streets, that they may be seen by men. Assuredly, I say to you, they have their reward. But you, **when you pray, go into your room**, and when you have **shut your door, pray to your Father** who is in the secret place; and your Father who sees **in secret** will reward you openly* (Matthew 6:5-6).

Do you make a regular habit to pray to God, alone? Are you willing to begin to do so now?

How Holy Spirit Empowers our Prayer Sessions

Along with the baptism of Holy Spirit, God empowers our prayer sessions as we learn to tap in to His revelation gifts. Just what are His gifts of revelation? The revelation gifts are supernatural gifts given to us that reveal something we would not know otherwise. These gifts of the Holy Spirit include the word of knowledge, the word of wisdom, and the discerning of spirits. These are mighty weapons of warfare when activated in times of intercession.

The Word of Wisdom

The word of wisdom is a message from the Lord about an event that will take place sometime in our future. The time frame isn't necessarily disclosed to us by the Lord, but can be. It may occur in the near future or far off into the distance of time.

We can read an illustration of this in Acts 27:21-26, where Paul admonishes the weary men with a word of wisdom that he receives from an angel revealing his future and the safety of the men on board the boat.

Many years ago, I was in a meeting when the pastor called me out and had a word of wisdom for me. This word was filled with events that were going to take place in my life—and it has happened as the spoken word of wisdom revealed. Please see my book *Greater than Magic,* Chapter 5, "Water and Wine," for in-depth details of this word of wisdom.

The Word of Knowledge

By a word of knowledge, we become privy to secret, hidden, or unknown information as the Spirit wills to inform us about present situations. The way I remember the difference between a word of wisdom and a word of knowledge is that the word "now" is in the word k**now**ledge. The time frame for a word of knowledge is now. A biblical account of this can be found in Acts 9:10-12 when Ananias receives a word of knowledge in the form of a vision from the Lord giving specific details and instructions on what is now happening in the life of Saul from Tarsus.

During times of intercession with my ministry assistant, the Lord continued to give to me words of knowledge about a spirit of chaos that was going to break out. Then one morning I awoke to a word of knowledge from Holy Spirit, "Prepare, chaos is breaking out now!" And just as He had warned in this word of knowledge in this prophetic dream, major chaos broke out the very next day. Please see my book *Greater Than Magic,* Chapter 5, "Water and Wine," for more details about this event in my life.

Discerning of Spirits

When people operate in this gift, they spiritually discern, perceive, detect, see, hear, and sense the spiritual realm around them. In Acts 16:16-18 we read how Paul, by discerning of spirits, was able to detect in a young girl a spirit of divination.

The discerning of spirits is a great supernatural gift of Holy Spirit; and when utilized in the realm of intercession, great revelations unravel before us. These revelations are the kind we would have no way of knowing if not for Holy Spirit revealing the hidden truths to us. And I believe, more than ever, with all the deception and lying taking place, we must have this gift of Holy Spirit operating in our lives. Please see my book, *Greater Than Magic,* Chapter 5, "Water and Wine," page 77.

Throughout this chapter we have seen how the Spirit of God is calling forth His people to revive and come alive again. In the next chapter we consider the healing power of God's love and how this love factor releases the tsunami wave of healing glory.

Faith Assignment

Get real with God this week, starting with today. Right now, pinpoint where you are spiritually, confess the sin of mediocre faith, and dedicate yourself to Him—free from the weight of this world. Worship Him, read and study His Word, and actually do what He tells you to do.

Questions to Ponder and Answer for Chapter 7: Revive and Come Alive Again

1. Why does the church in Ephesus fail the test?

   _____

   _____

   _____

2. The church in Smyrna is known as what?

   _____

   _____

   _____

3. With whom does God threaten to make war?

   _____

   _____

   _____

4. What are the sins of the church of Pergamum?

   _____

   _____

   _____

5. What church allows the Spirit of Jezebel to lead them?

_____

_____

_____

6. Which church is bound by a religious spirit?

_____

_____

_____

7. Why does the church of Philadelphia not receive a rebuke?

_____

_____

_____

8. What temperature is the church of Laodicea?

_____

_____

_____

9. Revival is a matter of what?

_____

_____

_____

10. Revival is not about what?

_____

_____

_____

11. What type of Christian does true spiritual revival resurrect?

_____

_____

_____

12. In Psalm 42:1-3, what does my soul thirst for?

_____

_____

_____

13. What do you need to grab on to and not let go?

_____

_____

_____

14. In Luke 11:11-13, what will the Father give to those who ask?

_____

_____

_____

15. In John 7:38-39, what will continually flow from your innermost being?

_____

_____

_____

16. Zechariah 4:6 says that it is not by what?

_____

_____

_____

17. In First Corinthians 1:10, Paul says that there should not be any what among us?

_____

_____

_____

18. In Matthew 6:5-6, what are you to do when you pray?

_____

_____

_____

Personal Assessment

You see the personal need to revive and come alive again. You have been wanting to, but have not known how to start over. You admit that your love for the Lord isn't where it once was or where it should be, but you are willing to begin again. You realize that Holy Spirit has a huge part to play in this matter. You admit that you are a little nervous about all of this, but you are open to the guidance of Holy Spirit. Oops! You may think to yourself, *I've been in this position before.* And I say don't get discouraged, this decision to move forward with your relationship with your Messiah only bumps you up a little bit sooner.

Group Discussion

With your group talk about the true revival that takes place within the heart of individuals and counterfeit moves of the human spirit. Discuss the revelation gifts and how the Lord may have used these to warn you of a current event. Offer to pray for one another's needs and end with a group prayer of repentance for being loveless for God.

Note

1. You can read this powerful testimony in my first work, *DARE to Believe,* Chapter 11, pages 175-193.

8

The Healing Power of God's Love

Word of the Lord

The Spirit of the Living God would say to you this day:

> Going to the Cross once was enough, but if I had to, I would willingly choose to do it again just for you. Most do not begin to understand the love that I have for each person on earth. My love is not based upon feelings, but upon the foundation of love—Me. All the suffering I endured was for your good. You are the beneficiary of My goodness. And all My benefits I give to you. These benefits are not temporal, they are eternal. My Word is forever, My promise is sure, and My will is sealed with My blood. Access the power of My blood.
>
> "I tell you the truth, your redemption cost Me everything. But I would willingly do it again, because that's how valuable you are to Me. The highest price had to be paid to redeem you back to Me. Nothing less than the best would do. There was no bartering—it was all or nothing.
>
> And I chose all for you. I gave all that I had—Myself for you. "Greater love has no one than this, than to lay down one's life for his friends. I tell you there is no greater love than this. And I lay down my life, not for one, but for all. And I would willingly do it again even if it were just for you. This is how

much I love you. With every drop of crimson red that I sweat in great anguish while I knelt in the Garden of Gethsemane, I willingly overcame because I thought of you and your victory. I did not protest as they ripped out My beard and tore apart My face; I bled, and My grace erased your shame.

As I willingly knelt at the whipping post, I endured the greatest of all suffering; and with the power of My blood I purchased your healing. Receive it, it belongs to you. You are cursed no more because I bore the piercing of that tremendous crown of thorns. And the power of My blood released you from the punishment of the curse—be free from it. As those nails were forcefully pounded through My hands, a great blessing poured through My blood for you. Live in the complete blessing—I freely give it to you.

With the crushing blow of that great nail through My feet to that old wooden Cross, I bequeath to you, through the mighty power of My blood, all My authority over satan and all of his wicked works—now walk in it. As they pierced My side and the remaining blood and water flowed from Me, I gave to you My plan of redemption and the opportunity to become born again. I give all of this to you, not out of obligation, but because I love you. And I would willingly do it again—just for you.

Thus saith the Lord your God, to you this day.

God's Word to Us

Whoa! Did you hear what God said to you through that word of the Lord? What tremendous love poured out of Him for our benefit! This tsunami wave of healing glory is empowered by the selfless love of God. His love is the reason for everything He has ever done for us. His entire plan of redemption is backed by His unconditional love. In fact, *"God demonstrates His own love toward us, in that while we were still sinners, Christ died for us"* (Romans 5:8). God's love is powerful and is packed with redemptive qualities that release us from all forms of bondage.

And all these waves within this tsunami wave of healing glory—worship, repentance, revelation truth, the Baptism of Holy Spirit, and the others yet to be discussed—are birthed from the wellspring of this amazing love of His.

Drench yourself in the supernatural power of His love. Be that dry sponge that soaks up every last drop of it until it just oozes out of you. You are so filled with His love, you can't help but share it to all around you. Everywhere you go you create puddles, streams, rivers and lakes of this tsunami wave of healing glory.

Teach Love at Home

We live in a loveless society—in a world filled with people who have not been loved, rather they have been used, abused, and seduced by others. Love has to be taught, and it starts in the home. A lot of what we see happening on the streets in the United States today is a direct result of what didn't happen in their homes as children. Many of these broken people grew up without a father figure. Or if a father or father figure was around, he was either abusive in some way or was present but absent of heart toward his family. Others grew up with mothers who were too caught up in their own selfishness that they really didn't raise their kids. Many times children are left to fend for themselves and miss something very crucial to a healthy life—love.

This is why we must raise our children in the ways of the Lord. Fill their hearts with love for God, and for all people, including themselves. When love can be seen, heard, practiced and felt within the home, it can be lived out anywhere, anytime.

Christian parent, rise up and love your children. Train them to know the difference between love and seduction. You can protect them from many hurts in life when you instill healthy boundaries in relationships. Teach them that their identity is in Christ, not in what others think about them. This way they will more likely have the confidence to stand up for what's right and say, "No!" to people who want to use them, abuse them, or destroy them with sinful ways.

Dexter's Passion to Raise Godly Sons

Dexter is a born-again believer in the Lord Jesus Christ, he is baptized in the Holy Spirit, and married to a wonderful Christian woman. They have two awesome sons who love Jesus. Together as a family they serve the Lord. Dexter really has a wonderful life, but it wasn't always this way for him. I asked Dexter, my friend, intercessor, and a member of my prayer team, to share his story with us. And to dig deep into his heart and tell us why it is so important to him to raise his two sons in the name of the Lord during such turbulent times. Let's read what he has to say.

"What are you looking at, four eyes?" and "Where did you get that fake 'Members Only' jacket?"

Those were the words that would often greet Dexter when he went to school as a young kid. It really didn't matter what he was wearing because the crowd had already decided nothing Dexter did, wore, or said was good enough. He just never seemed to fit in. Because of this and the negative words Dexter internalized from his peers, he endured many years of low self-esteem issues because he didn't understand his true identity.

But looking back, Dexter realized that him not fitting in due to rejection was part of God's protection. Nevertheless, during that time he was determined to do whatever he could to become part of the "in crowd." Dexter wanted to fit in at all cost, even if it required making unwise and reckless decisions that oftentimes caused embarrassment or disappointment for his parents.

God in His patience, mercy, and grace, allowed Dexter to remain on this journey until college. He tried out for the football team as a way to meet girls and get into the in crowd. One day one of the stars of the team invited him to his room with another player for a Bible study. He only said yes because he thought it was a way to get the guy's approval. Little did he know he would truly find that he had the approval of the One who kept him from falling when he accepted Christ as his Savior. That day Dexter left that dorm room a changed man.

He returned home from school, a new creation. With his new-found relationship with the Lord, Dexter had more questions about the Bible than the pastor was willing to answer. Because of this, he often felt excluded and ostracized because of his intense curiosity about the Bible. This was yet another time when he felt he didn't fit in.

Dexter later left that church and attended another church where he began to grow—and where he would later find his future wife, Tiffany. As he matured in the Word of God, he was often asked to lead the church Bible study and Sunday school classes. Dexter hid a very dark secret from everyone—he struggled with an addiction to pornography. Although he was in denial about it, this spirit of pornography had a strong hold on him. In fact, this addiction weakened his marriage and caused a lot of hurt and pain once his wife discovered it.

After complete deliverance from the stronghold of pornography addiction, Dexter committed that when he and his wife had children, he would break this generational curse, empower and equip his sons with the Scriptures and resources to uplift the Kingdom, and always expect miracles, signs, and wonders. He also wanted his boys to realize, early in life, that what the enemy used to torment him—trying to fit in, battling with low self-esteem, and pornography addiction—they would be able to overcome and avoid through a strong, intimate relationship with Jesus Christ.

For this reason, Dexter is adamant about consistently giving his sons a clear understanding of their identity in Christ—that they were created not to fit in, but to stand out as children of the Most High. He taught them that God has a wonderful plan for them, which is much greater and bigger than the plans they could have for themselves.

A Declaration of Faith to Teach Your Children

Children are more stable when they know that they belong to something good, a healthy family and a Bible-believing church, and that their safety is valued. Being a member of God's family gives them a sense of belonging and security in the midst of a throw-away society, that easily "unfriends" at the push of a button. Teach them this simple declaration of faith and say it together at the start of the day and at the end of the night to help them feel secure in following their own convictions and do what's right.

I am loved (Romans 5:5). I am adopted by God (Romans 8:15). He is my Father, and I am His child (2 Corinthians 6:18). I am not alone (Hebrews 13:5). God is always with me (Matthew 28:20). I am not a stranger or a foreigner, but a citizen of God's Kingdom with other believers; I am a member of God's household (Ephesians 2:19), the household of faith (Galatians 6:10).

I choose my friends wisely (Proverbs 12:26). God looks at the heart and so do I (1 Samuel 16:7). I will not be bullied nor will I bully others (Proverbs 31:8-9). I have integrity (Proverbs 10:9). I am strong and courageous (Deuteronomy 31:6). I will not be afraid (Isaiah 41:10). With Christ's strength I can do all things (Philippians 4:13). I make good decisions (James 1:5). I will not be naïve (Proverbs 14:15). I am a friend of God (John 15:15).

Why Do Bad Things Happen to Good People?

If God is so loving, do you ever wonder why bad things happen to good people? People want to know the answer to that question, and the religious community doesn't seem to be able to give the real reason—but God's people can. Jesus gives us the answer to this question in Scripture. Jesus says in John 16:33, *"These things I have spoken to you, that in Me you may have peace. In the world you will have tribulation; but **be of good cheer**, I have overcome the world."*

Tribulation, difficult times, entered our earth when Adam and Eve decided to rebel against God and His ways. This original sin opened the door to satan and his evil ways and allowed corruption to enter into our world and into the human body as well.

Did you notice that in the midst of difficulties Jesus says to be of good cheer? This does not mean that we are to be happy because we are facing hardships, but because of what He did for us at Calvary. We can now walk in victory despite sufferings.

God did not create people to suffer, but sometimes we do because we live in a fallen world.

Who Causes Suffering?

The next logical question to follow the first one is, "So, if it is not God's plan for people to suffer, then who is responsible?" Again, God gives us the answer in His Word to this painful topic of who is responsible. In John 10:10 (NIV), Jesus clearly describes satan's intentions, *"The thief comes only to steal and kill and destroy; I have come that they may have life, and have it to the full."* God is not responsible for all the evil around us, satan is. And the devil is hell-bent upon our destruction. Jesus calls him a thief who comes to steal God's promises from us.

We also need to accept the fact that while yes, satan is the one behind all evil, we too have a part to play in many of the messes in our lives. God gives us free will, and with this free will comes great responsibility to make right choices in life. With free will we can sin if we want to, but sin is fun for only a season, then we eventually have to reap what we sow. James 1:14 (AMP) explains it to us this way, *"But each one is tempted when he is dragged away, enticed and baited [to commit sin] by his own [worldly] desire (lust, passion)."*

Odessa's Story

I was raised in church. I remember loving Jesus and loving church. When I was ten years old, my stepfather began sexually abusing me. I remember how carefree I was before this and how after this, I was filled with fear, guilt, and shame. He threatened to kill my mother if I told anyone, so I kept this secret. It was very confusing to me, because he also attended church, was a gospel singer, and gospel music was played in our home a lot. I always prayed and cried out to Jesus to protect me, my sisters, and our mom.

School was my safe place, and my grades were pretty good until my stepfather began to even defile that. He had pornographic magazines and would force me to "read" a word that he said he couldn't pronounce, and then, as he'd turn the page, I would see sexual bondage scenes.

One day, I decided to tell someone who was connected to the county. They took me to Social Services to report this, but Social Services did not know what to do. They called him to ask if what I was saying was true. When he said, "No," that was that. But because I told, he no longer had that hold on me. He beat me and treated me badly, but stopped the sexual abuse. Silence and fear seem to be necessary for sexual offenders and pedophiles to hold one captive.

Everything about me had changed. Sadly, several of my stepfather's friends also began to molest me (I think because they knew what he was doing and getting away with). What I knew to be true was that I was not to have sex until I was married, so I tried desperately to hold on to my virtue. I knew I had done nothing to cause these men to do this to me.

I loved Jesus, and I knew He loved me. I prayed, cried, waited, and believed Jesus would come or send me a "Charles Bronson" to rescue me (I had just seen one of his tough-guy movies). I never blamed God for what was happening. At a young age, I understood that Jesus never sinned, yet suffered and died because of my sins, so who was I to live without suffering?

Years later, our mother left this man, but we still lived from that place of brokenness, fear, and shame. I hated who I felt I was in the eyes of God. It nearly destroyed me, because I did not want Jesus to see me.

When I graduated from high school and my twin sister joined the military, I had a very difficult time emotionally. I would just think and think and think. How could I possibly please God now that I was "damaged goods"? I literally had fear of living, because I felt I was no longer usable to God, and I also had fear of dying and going to hell. This was a lie of satan, but my identity in Christ had been completely stolen.

As I began to live as a young adult, I was broken, but I could now make my own decisions. I met someone who introduced me to a life of prostitution. This would become my secret life for a season, as I convinced myself I was okay, for now I was in the company of other women who had similar experiences and understood me. As we began to trust one another, we began to share our stories. For many of the ladies, this was the first time they had ever told anyone. Though I found a measure of healing there, God, in His love and faithfulness, would not leave me in that life. I started thinking about Jesus every day, all day, and one night I cried out to God and said, "God, if You are real, show Yourself to me. I feel as though I am floating in space, belonging nowhere and to no one." I could not be consoled.

A few weeks after I cried out to God, I learned that I was pregnant by the guy I was dating. (He did not yet know about my secret life.) I decided to leave the life of prostitution and have my child. My boyfriend did not want to have a child with me, so I was to be a single mother. I did not have a plan, but I felt this child was God's answer to the cry of my heart.

I named him "Bronson," and God would teach me so much about His love and provision for me through Bronson—so much so that I began seeking God again. I realized I had no skills, no job experience, nothing. God gave me a supernatural knowledge of computers, and I was able to get a job building computers. From building computers to selling software, this is still the provision of God for my family today.

God introduced me to a loving, powerful, anointed woman of God, who would invest in me, for the sake of Christ. Though I still lived an unholy life, she stood by me and led me to where I received the baptism of the Holy Spirit, because she knew I needed God's power to overcome. And she helped get me to a place in God where I believed and accepted His forgiveness for myself. My identity in Christ was being restored. This is when I began to breathe again.

After sitting under good biblical teaching at my church, I got a revelation of Christ in us (me), the hope of glory, and I began to live a life of purpose. Jesus has filled me to overflow with His love. Because my sins, which are many, are forgiven, I love much. My heart's desire is that everyone come to know

God's love for themselves. We suffer from identity crises, but once our identity is found in Him, we may live a whole and holy life.

I delight myself in the Lord, and I trust Him to grant me the desires of my heart. I now have a husband who loves the Lord, and we have seven children (combined) and seventeen grandchildren. My sons are the first generation, in what I know of my family's lineage, to have lived without sexual abuse. Jesus, in His great power and love, has broken this curse.

My husband was homeless at one time and is now a homeowner. I love and live Jesus out loud. I am wholly His. I am nothing apart from Him. His redemptive grace is ever being displayed in our lives.

God has even blessed me with the opportunity to work with my friend Amy, ministering His heart to women in the sex industry. The message of God's heart is clear. These women are seen, valued, purposed, and loved by God. He alone is Redeemer. He works all things together for the good of those who love Him and are called according to His purposes. Life happens, but God's call and purposes don't change. He changes not. As I once heard a godly person say, "God's original intention is His final decision." We can trust Him to heal us completely and place us in the very center of His will. For this, I am humbled and grateful. I am redeemed.

I share my friend Odessa's testimony with you and how her ashes of sorrow and hopelessness were healed by Jesus alone, and transformed into His beauty. The spirit of heaviness fell off and she found joy once again. You can find this healing and joy too.

So many people are in need of inner healing, like Odessa fought to find. This present world is filled with angry, confused, fearful, and hurting people, which is often the reason for physical illness. We the children of the living God can minister healing to their souls (mind and emotions). Ministering to a broken soul often releases the physical healing they need.

The key to reaping the great end times harvest is learning to operate in the fullness of His divine love for all people. This love is within us and is what we were reborn with—the unconditional love of God. The Spirit of God is waiting on us to unleash the power of His love to this sin-ridden world.

Are you willing to reach out and help someone who has been broken in life? Be honest with yourself and with God.

A Prayer of Faith for the Abused

In the name of our great Redeemer and Healer, Yeshua, the Messiah, I speak peace to your soul that you see yourself as God sees you—redeemed, cleansed, healed, and made whole. You see yourself in His mirror image; as Jesus is, so are you on this earth. No longer do you call yourself a victim—you are an overcomer, even more than a conqueror. By faith, you can take back by force what satan has stolen from you—your love, hope, and joy. I pray for His courage to rise up within you and you face the past through the eyes of your Savior and Lord—forgiven and forgotten.

I declare in the power of His might that this is the day that the Lord has made and you will rejoice and be glad in it. You will dare to pick up joy and clothe your innermost being with it. You cling to the biblical truth that the joy of the Lord is your strength. No longer will you blend into the wall and try to hide in the shame of the past—you will rise up in these last days delivered and set free from the clutches of the enemy. Allow yourself to be wrapped in the love of your Lord this day and forevermore, amen.

Who Does He Say We Are?

We've read a couple of real-life stories of people suffering from not understanding their true identity in their Messiah. This world is filled with broken, confused, depressed, and lonely people. Let us look to the Author and Finisher of our faith to discover who He says we are. I believe if we will forsake what the world says about us and take to heart our God-given identity and confess His description about us, we will heal from low self-esteem.

God says we are:

- A chosen generation, a royal priesthood, a holy nation, and His special people (1 Peter 2:9)
- A new creation (2 Corinthians 5:17) created in His image (Genesis 1:27)
- His workmanship (Ephesians 2:10)
- God's temple (1 Corinthians 3:16)
- More than conquerors (Romans 8:37)
- Beloved, born of God (1 John 4:7)
- Fearfully and wonderfully made (Psalm 139:14)
- Citizens of Heaven (Philippians 3:20)
- Children of God (Galatians 3:26 NIV)
- The Body of Christ (1 Corinthians 12:27)
- The righteousness of God (2 Corinthians 5:21)
- Branches of the Vine (John 15:5)
- Children of God (John 1:12)
- Heirs of God and joint heirs with Christ (Romans 8:17)
- Friends of God (John 15:15)

- Valuable (Luke 12:7)
- Forgiven of our sins and cleansed us from all unrighteousness (1 John 1:9)

Choose to believe this day who God says you are. Forsake the negative and lying spirit of satan. Quote these godly images over yourself—stop believing the negative images of the world. Trust God and allow yourself to be set free. Amen.

The Greatest Cure for Mental Illness

The greatest cure for mental illness is not more drugs—the cure is the unconditional love of God and the power of His love found within the pages of His Word—the Holy Bible. I believe much of what the world refers to mental illness is demonic oppression or possession. I also believe that most deliverance will come by renewing the soul (the mind and emotions) with God's healing Word. The Bible tells us in Isaiah 26:3 (AMP):

> You [God] *keep in perfect peace and constant peace the one whose mind is steadfast [that is, committed and focused on You—in both inclination and character], because he trusts and takes refuge in You [with hope and confident expectation].*

Do you need this perfect peace operating in your life today? If so, you're not alone, many of God's people are suffering from attacks on their mind and emotions. But I am a firm believer in the power of God's Word. If we will keep our thoughts focused on the love of God and His promises, His perfect peace will belong to us.

We are responsible to take control of our thoughts. We are not to allow them to wander off into territory where we don't belong. Proverbs 4:23 warns us to *"Keep your heart with all diligence, for out of it spring the issues of life."* Philippians 4:6-7 (NIV) teaches us how to guard the innermost thoughts of our hearts. It admonishes us in this way:

Do not be anxious about anything, but in every situation, by prayer and petition, with thanksgiving, present your requests to God. And the peace of God, which transcends all understanding, will guard your hearts and your minds in Christ Jesus.

What have you been thinking about? In what arena are your thoughts dwelling? Your heart will eventually follow after your deep inner thoughts. And once they get inside your heart, your actions will follow after them.

If your thoughts are dwelling in sexual sins, your actions will follow after those unclean thoughts. And if you allow yourself to dwell in these dark places, you will become enslaved to sexual perversion of all types.

If you watch satanic movies or read books about the occult, you open yourself up to the realm of the devil and he will make sure his demons take control of your mind and emotions.

Drugs and alcohol cause your spiritual filters to fail you, and you become easy prey to satan's demonic strongholds. You will either become oppressed or possessed with demons.

If you are unequally yoked with an unbeliever whether in marriage, business, or friendship, you put your soul (mind and emotions) in jeopardy of transferring of spirits. The same spirit controlling them will enter and inhabit your domain.

No matter the unwelcoming situation you have found yourself in, there is hope for deliverance and healing in God's Word. But you have to choose to be free, and make quality decisions on a daily basis to get free. If you are standing in proxy for a loved one, you have to fight for the deliverance and for the freedom of this person by prayer and fasting and standing on the promises of God.

My son, give attention to my words; incline your ear to my sayings. Do not let them depart from your eyes; keep them in the midst of your heart; for they are life to those who find them, and health to all their flesh (Proverbs 4:20-22).

I believe that most deliverance will simply come by staying in the Word of God. Living a lifestyle of reading and studying, meditating on the promises of God, speaking these promises aloud over yourself, and doing what it says to do brings deliverance. If you will do what I just wrote here, you will find your freedom. Those who are further into the bondage of satan will need others to fight for them.

Jesus says in Matthew 17:21 concerning certain types of demon possession, *"this kind does not go out except by prayer and fasting."*

There are times in life when our hearts are overwhelmed with sorrow and grief, and that unspeakable pain permeates one's being. It is times like these that we must find the way to heal.

Allow yourself to become vulnerable to family and friends who truly want to help in your time of need. They love you and care about you. You will find you do not have to explain much, they already know and understand the situation. They desire to be a support beam for you to lean on when you feel weak.

And then there are those unexpected people God will speak to concerning you to find a way to reach out to you to also help carry you through. Don't be closed-minded, you may find a rich jewel in a new friendship that will bless you in your time of sorrow.

Then there are times when the people around you are not able to reach inside and heal the deep wound of sorrow. This is when you need to choose to grab hold of the Spirit of the Living God for help, inner healing, peace and strength that does not come from this world.

There are different levels of healing, and God uses people to help us through difficult trials in this life; and then there is a deep inner healing that only God alone can heal. We have to choose to wipe off the ashes of sorrow and allow Him to wash us with His atoning blood and make us whole again.

Take a Stand in Love for the Vulnerable

We are called to protect the weak and the vulnerable. We cannot repeat the sins of the past, such as in the days of Hitler and the annihilation of the Jews, or continue the sins of the present and devalue our elderly population, or disregard the physically imperfect people, or discard the unwanted children. We must stand up for what's right in the eyes of the Lord and stand for life—for all lives truly matter to our Lord.

> *Rescue the weak and needy; rescue them from the hand of the wicked* (Psalm 82:4 AMP).

Years ago, back in the days when my family lived in Minnesota, I was faced with a crowd of bullies who were being cruel to a young man with mental challenges. This group of men appeared to be of the same family—several generations.

And let me insert this here, if you will, I tell you people have to be taught to hate, and satan is behind brutality. But with our new nature, the recreated, born-again spirit, we are birthed from the heart of the Father—love. Love is a supernatural power that overrides the powers of hate and cruelty. In our everyday lives with everyday encounters, we are called to love as the Father loves—unconditionally and without partiality.

Allow me to continue to weave this story. I was a young Christian wife and mother at this time and had our three kids out for a special luncheon with me after the morning church service. And here I found myself unexpectedly in the middle of a vulnerable stranger's problem.

The love of God within me was outraged by the cruelty of the grown men. Publicly they were insulting and taunting the young man who didn't understand that he lacked the proper funds to pay for his meal. He was left to fend for himself against this pack of vicious wolves.

Now I had a choice to make. I could be the passive Christian and keep my mouth shut and allow the management to handle the situation. Or I could be proactive and use my faith, which is fueled by the love of God, and do something. I chose to get involved and help this vulnerable man. Although our finances were tight at this time, I quietly stepped forward in the midst of the evil men, reached into my purse, and said to the cashier, "Please allow me to pay for his meal." Then I led the man to the buffet line and stood my ground against these low-life bullies.

We have to be willing to bring back God's law and order into the land—our nations and communities. This is the type of love in action that the Father is requiring His children to take. Protect the vulnerable people of this world in the name of the Lord.

And I'm telling you, the act of lovingkindness, as small as it was, silenced the men in their tracks. I believe it highlighted their immature and evil nature. And they didn't say one word—they stood there with their shame exposed. There are golden opportunities all around us to stop the enemy's violent attacks and glorify Abba Father.

I understand that times have changed and have become very violent and dangerous for us all. But we, the Church, have to address these issues today, and bravely take a stand for the vulnerable around us.

What about our elderly? They need us to protect them. They protected us when we were young and vulnerable, now it's our turn to do the same for them. It grieves me deeply to see young people viciously attack our elderly population. It's a cowardly act of terrorism.

The elderly hold the keys to the past. It is such an obvious attack of satan to try to wipe out our connection to our history, whether good or bad. Wisdom is gained by time and experience. And our seniors possess both of these gifts.

I loved my grandparents, and I miss them to this day. I have their photos on my walls and I remember the lessons in life that they imparted to me.

Teach your children to respect their elders and to glean wisdom from their many stories of the past. Provide the opportunity for your children to hold these treasures in their hearts.

What is the biblical view of our elderly?

Wisdom belongs to the aged, and understanding to the old (Job 12:12 NLT).

You shall rise before the gray headed and honor the presence of an old man, and fear your God: I am the Lord (Leviticus 19:32).

Do not rebuke an older man, but exhort him as a father, younger men as brothers, older women as mothers, younger women as sisters, with all purity (1 Timothy 5:1-2).

Another vulnerable group that I will again mention but from another aspect of the issue, is the slaughter of innocent unborn babies while in their mother's wombs—abortion—and now the murderous attack against defenseless children while on the birthing table. Although President Trump signed an Executive Order in October 2020 protecting babies who are born prematurely or survived an abortion, there is no guarantee that the action will carry as much weight as it should in the medical community or legislatures.

Psalm 139:13-16 (AMP) tells us just how our Creator feels about the unborn baby in the womb.

For You formed my innermost parts; You knit me [together] in my mother's womb. I will give thanks and praise to You, for I am fearfully and wonderfully made; wonderful are Your works, and my soul knows it very well. My frame was not hidden from You, when I was being formed in secret, and intricately and skillfully formed [as if embroidered with many colors] in the depths of the earth. Your eyes have seen my unformed substance; and in Your book were all written the days that were appointed for me, when as yet there was not one of them [even taking shape].

How does our God feel about killing innocent babies?

- It's one of the seven sins He hates the most—the shedding of innocent blood (see Proverbs 6:17).
- God's Word is perfectly clear in Exodus 20:13, the sixth commandment states, "You shall not murder."

Abortion is wrong. It is not to be tolerated within the Christian Church. We must speak up and minister hope and help to women who have found themselves in an unexpected pregnancy. Offer a real solution to those who don't want to keep their baby—adoption. And help them through this solution of love. We also need to minister inner healing to the many women who have already been damaged by past abortions. They need counseling to help forgive themselves and to overcome the guilt and the shame that they suffer on a daily basis.

I also believe, as frightening as it might be, that we are to stand in the gap, even be willing to risk our lives for those being attacked on the streets of our nations today. Proverbs 24:11 (AMP) says outright, *"Rescue those who are being taken away to death, and those who stagger to the slaughter, Oh hold them back [from their doom]!"*

I don't know where you stand in your faith, but I believe in the power of the blood of Christ to protect us from our enemy. And I believe now is the time for the Body of Christ to activate our faith to the highest level of total trust and surrender, and allow Jesus, our Defender and Protector, to push back the enemy. Call for the angels of God to show up (literally appear) and fight for us.

The Love Factor

Along with personal revival as discussed in the last chapter, the love factor of life will cause this tsunami wave of healing glory to break loose. And just what is the love factor causing this breakthrough? The love of Jesus Christ.

Imagine yourself filling up the bathtub, the water is running. Then you get sidetracked and forget the water is running. When the water reaches the brim, it can't help but overflow onto the surrounding floor, and then it continues to flow from one room to another. And before you realize it the foundation is completely saturated.

Now picture yourself and that water as being one, and the water is the love factor in your life. This love factor is the love of God filling you up to the point that you just can't contain it any longer.

This is what God desires of His people—for us to be willing vessels that He can pour His love into. He wants us to forget about turning the faucet off, that way we allow His living waters to continuously pour through us and His love just naturally overflows to those around us.

> *And may the Lord make your love for one another and for all people grow and overflow, just as our love for you overflows* (1 Thessalonians 3:12 NLT).

Love Goes the Extra Mile

A beautiful woman from New York had been suffering from ALS, which kept her bound to a wheelchair for twelve years. She could not stand or walk on her own; in fact, many of the physical things she had once been able to do, she could no longer do on her own. In the natural, her physical being was slowly dying.

But her husband heard that I was going to be ministering in Salisbury, North Carolina, and he decided to put his faith into action—faith fueled by the love of God for his wife. They drive many miles so she can attend the healing conference.

As the power of Holy Spirit is being released, the man brings his wife to the front of the room. The tsunami wave of healing glory flows over his wife, and she stood up and out of that chair that she has been bound to for twelve years. She took her first steps in many years. The congregation went wild and we all cheered this woman on. She walked back and forth for all to see. Her body straightened out and she gained strength with every step.

This is a compelling example of how love goes the extra mile. Like the husband's love, Luke 5:19 tells of a group who went the extra mile for a sick friend: *"And when they could not find how they might bring him in, because of the crowd, they went up on the housetop and let him down with his bed through the tiling into the midst before Jesus."* And we read on how the Messiah healed the man.

Love goes out of its way to bring the sick for healing. Let's be willing to go the extra mile to release the healing power of the Lord into desperately needy people today.

> *Beloved,* ***let us love one another, for love is of God;*** *and everyone who loves is born of God and knows God. He who does not love does not know God, for* ***God is love*** *(1 John 4:7-8).*

We have taken the time to consider the great healing power of the love of God, and how this love factor is absolutely necessary to release the tsunami wave of healing glory in these extremely trying times. In addition to what we've discussed in this chapter about the healing power of God's love, we the Church can no longer be silent during this chaotic time in history. The Church must find her voice again.

Prayer

Abba Father, again I am challenged within my spirit to activate my faith for Your glory. I know there are vulnerable people all around me. And so I bravely ask, Holy Spirit, highlight their needs to me. Show me what You would have me to do to express to them Your unconditional love toward them. In Your most holy name, I pray, amen.

Faith Assignment

Pray to the Father in the name of Jesus and ask Holy Spirit to lead you to a vulnerable person in need of your loving support. Step out of your comfort zone and lend a helping hand. Remember, there are golden opportunities all around us to glorify our Abba Father.

Questions to Ponder and Answer for Chapter 8: The Healing Power of God's Love

1. What type of society do you live in?

    _____

    _____

    _____

2. Many people grew up without what type of figure?

    _____

    _____

    _____

3. Some fathers are present but absent of what?

    _____

    _____

    _____

4. Christian parents need to train their children to know the difference between what?

_____

_____

_____

5. Children are more stable when they know what?

_____

_____

_____

6. If God is so loving, why do bad things happen to good people?

_____

_____

_____

7. Who is responsible for suffering?

_____

_____

_____

8. What is the greatest cure for mental illness?

_____

_____

_____

9. Who are you called to protect?

_____

_____

_____

10. What will cause the tsunami wave of healing glory to break loose?

_____

_____

_____

11. Why do you need to be willing to go the extra mile?

_____

_____

_____

Personal Assessment

Did I grow up with a loving father and mother figure? If not, have I healed from my past childhood situation? Am I training my children to know the difference between true love and seduction? Am I suffering from mental illness? If so, am I willing to be discipled in God's unconditional love that is found in the pages of His Word—the Holy Bible? Are there vulnerable people in my life? Do I take a stand to protect and defend the vulnerable people in my life? Am I willing to go the extra mile and release the healing power of Jesus Christ into the lives of those around me?

Group Discussion

Have an open discussion with your group about defending the vulnerable in your community. Talk about different scenarios and how you might handle them in a loving and courageous manner to defend them in the name of the Lord.

9

We Cannot Remain Silent

Word of the Lord

The Lord God would say to you this day,

Lean not unto your own understanding. In all of your ways acknowledge Me and I will direct your paths. Faithfulness is not a quality that I overlook. I honor its carriers in every way. Keep your eyes fixed upon Me and not upon the circumstances around you.

The enemy is viciously attacking My servants; do not allow yourself to be counted among his victims. For greater am I in you than this serpent of old. Old are his ways, but My ways are older than his, he has nothing over you unless you allow him to—don't allow him to take you down and your ministry that I have given to you.

You are living in the last days; things will get tough, but My people are called to be even tougher! Not in your own strength, but by the strength of My Spirit. I created you to be bold, not timid; your courage comes from Me. The more you know Me, the bolder you will be.

Strength and encouragement I give to you. Rest in Me; know that the game plan for these last days are different from what they were yesterday. Learn to listen to My voice and begin to

> rejoice as My plans are not to harm or to destroy you—they are to prosper you in the power of My grace. And it is by My grace that you will conclude your race; and at the finish line each of Mine will hear My Father say, "Well done, good and faithful servant." This is the love of the Father toward you this day—Jesus, your Lord.

Many ministries basically came to a screeching halt during the 2020 pandemic and the near shutdown of the world's economy. Many pastors were beside themselves with confusion, fear, and worry. One day they had viable ministries, yet within a brief time they along with the entire world were closed until further notice.

I have stated from the beginning of this work when I first shared the vision of the tsunami wave of healing that along with this tsunami wave of healing glory is an undertow of strong doubt and unbelief. One of the strong undertows rising is persecution to drown out the voice of the Church—to keep her silent.

The enemy knows the power of the words of the Church, he has been fighting them ever since Adam was created. And now he has millions of spiritual Adams and Eves to contend with. So now he is going after the jugular vein—the supernatural power of the spoken word. It would be a whole lot easier for him to go about his dirty business if our mouths were gagged.

Dear reader, we are the Church, and history has proven we cannot be stopped—but the pressure of persecution can silence us if we let it. Times of persecution are upon us, which is all the more reason to decide once and for all not to be silent!

It's disheartening to witness how easy it is to silence the majority of the Church. This silence reveals much about how we see ourselves, and what we actually believe and don't believe.

With the outbreak of COVID-19, we were told to prevent the spread of this disease by not gathering together for a short time. From a good heart to protect one another we complied.

But then we began to see the world declare what they thought were "essential services" such as liquor stores and abortion clinics that remained open, but church services were considered nonessential. Even though society has been on a moral decline and we are often the ones people in need come to for help, as the reports of depression, domestic abuse, and suicide began to increase, our doors remained officially closed.

Have you considered the possible reasons why the world says the Church is nonessential? Beside the fact that the devil is a liar and he hates us—the true Church. This is a humbling thought and something we need to take with us to prayer. We must learn how to become the essential component that our communities can't live without. Allow Holy Spirit to incubate a plan about how to reach the lost before it's too late.

Some churches were told they were allowed to open if they practiced social distancing, wear masks, and significantly decrease the number of people permitted to attend services. We again complied with all the demands.

Hey, let's stop and take a good look at all of this. Number one, how can the state government tell us we cannot assemble? Where in the Bible does God give them this right over us? In fact, the very first amendment to the Constitution of the United States, acknowledges the "right of the people to assemble peaceably" and freedom of speech. The First Amendment was adopted in 1791 as part of the Bill of Rights, which are the first ten amendments, providing constitutional protection for certain individual liberties including freedoms of speech, assembly, and worship!

And now as I write this, some state governments are saying we can't sing during our worship services. I pray the Church in the United States will lift up her voice and say, "Enough is enough!" and take back our religious freedom to worship. I don't see anywhere in God's Word that we are to keep silent, in fact I see the opposite.

Many know the story of the prophet Jonah. If you don't know it, open your Bible to the Old Testament and read the Book of Jonah. He was called by the Lord to go to the people of Nineveh, but he didn't care enough about the people to deliver a message of repentance to the people. He disobeyed the Lord and foolishly thought he could outrun God and escape his destiny. His selfish spirit landed him in the sea and into the belly of a great fish. Jonah eventually repented and went to Nineveh where the people accepted his message and accepted the Lord.

Are we like Jonah, uncaring and merciless for the lost and hurting people of this world? Do we want to go where we want to go, and do the things we want to do? Do we think too highly of ourselves and refuse to go and speak on the behalf of the Lord because the people are too lowly for us? Or the place He wills to send us is below our self-centered status? Is the missionary calling, whether on the other side of the world or in our own community, too insignificant for our vanity? Have we become too important in our own eyes to do the work of the Lord?

If you only knew what I have witnessed hit the mission field in the name of the Lord, you would be appalled! And in the same breath, let us take a good hard look into the mirror of the Word of God and judge our own heart motives and ask ourselves, "Why are we not speaking up?" What is the truth behind our silence?

During this overreach of the worldly kingdom into the matters of God's Kingdom, now more than ever the Church needs to stand strong—for Him and for all His children. Let's pray, "Father God, forgive the Body of Christ. We don't fully understand the damage our silence has created, the lives lost to the devil and eternal damnation. Forgive us for losing our first love and true purpose on earth today. Help us to redeem the time we have wasted and the souls we have neglected to impact. In Jesus' name we pray, amen."

Take a Stand

Ah, you may think to yourself, *I don't need to say anything, this will pass.* So you think kicking the can down the road will make the enemy stop his attacks of persecution? No, he won't.

I too believe the pandemic will pass, but what will be the next fear and death tactic the enemy will use against us? He got away with it this time, and he is not going to stop. He will keep pulling the same strings as long as we allow him to get away with it. After all, he caused us to stop gathering together and from listening to the Word preached in a public setting. Corporate worship within local churches came to a screeching halt—and we accepted it all without much of a fight.

The fight to worship God goes back into Exodus. In chapter 7 we can read about the fight the Israelites had with pharaoh, the governing official, for their right to worship their God. Pharaoh, who thought he was a god, was lording over them with his will to keep them enslaved to his ungodly power. But God sent Moses to fight for them, and we read how God's people won back their right to worship.

We are in the same battle, friend. We have allowed ourselves to become governed by the ungodly. And the Spirit of the Lord says, "No more of this! Use your voice for My glory."

Let's look to Psalm 107:2 and remind ourselves about speaking up for ourselves. This Scripture says what we are to voice, ***"Let the redeemed of the Lord say so, whom He has redeemed from the hand of the enemy."*** We are the redeemed of the Lord and we are to declare this over ourselves—and to those who need to hear the good news of Jesus.

Jesus Christ, our Redeemer, bought and paid in full our deliverance, forgiveness, and freedom with His precious blood. We fully deserve the penalties of sin and the consequences of those sins—sickness, disease, death, hell and damnation. But by the power of His love, He shed His blood to set us free from these eternal consequences.

Our enemy, satan, works hard to condemn us so that we are unable to access our authority over him, and take down his wickedness around us. But our ever-loving Jesus nailed all requirements against us to the Cross.

> *Having wiped out the handwriting of requirements that was against us, which was contrary to us. And He has taken it out of the way, having nailed it to the cross* (Colossians 2:14).

When we begin to declare God's holy status over ourselves—"I am redeemed"—instead of what the enemy or the religious community would have us say about ourselves—"I'm just an old sinner saved by grace"—we take on the battle cry of the Victorious One who rightly declares that we are more than conquerors. In declaring these words over ourselves we create the atmosphere of victory around ourselves.

When we voice our authority and victory over satan, it scares him to death. He knows that we are no longer pushovers and that we know the true battle plan. His false reports against us don't stand a chance to destroy us. He is the one on the run—not us.

Why the Church Is Silent

I woke up to the voice of Holy Spirit speaking to me this morning about why the Church is silent and the dangers that silence will create for us. Let's discuss these issues now, and then do something about it.

In all honesty, I think the main reason the Church is silent about the injustices taking place against us is the fear of going under financially. There is a fear of losing the support of the members and not having enough to pay the bills or salaries. How about the fear that if they fight the unfair treatment by their local authorities, they could lose their 501c3 status, or be fined for not complying with the antichrist spirit rising up against the Church.

The Holy Bible tells us that we either serve God or we serve mammon (money), and that we cannot serve both at the same time. Let's read the words from our Lord about this now in Matthew 6:24, *"No one can serve two masters; for either he will hate the one and love the other, or else he will be loyal to the one and despise the other. You cannot serve God and mammon* [money]."

Yes, it takes financial means to run the established Church, to pay the mortgage, rent, utilities, and salaries for the pastors and other workers. That's a normal part of life, but setting these things aside for just one moment, please, let us focus on this portion of Scripture. We need to ask ourselves the hard question, "Who are we going to serve?" Are we going to serve our Lord and Savior, no matter what that will cost us? Are we willing to serve Him even if it means we lose our tax-free status? Will we remain faithful to the faith even if it costs us our buildings? Or will we continue to bow to the spirit of mammon and continue on this path of evil governing control over us that wants to silence our Christian conservative voices?

If we remain silent, we will lose all of our religious freedoms that have been secured under our constitutional rights as being one nation, under God.

We are at a crossroads and we have to make our choice. Who is it going to be? Jesus Christ or the spirit of mammon.

We Are in the Midst of a Battle

We're living in perilous times that are coming at us in waves of destruction. The spirit of fear and the spirit of death are behind these destructive waves that are ramping up their efforts against us to steal, kill, and destroy in every way possible. These efforts have attacked us in the form of pestilence, disease, pandemics, deadly weather, and terroristic attacks against everyday people. Truthfully, people around the world have been through great suffering brought on by the spirit of fear, the forerunner to the spirit of death.

The enemy is trying to wear down the will of the people, especially God's people, to adhere to his wickedness. The devil's army is trying to steal our spiritual legal rights, like with Adam in the Garden of Eden. (See Genesis 3.) But do we allow that serpent of old, the devil, to steal our spiritual rights from us today? Jesus Christ, our Deliverer and Savior, redeemed us from satan and all his wicked works. Jesus paid the ransom that was necessary by His redemptive blood, and returned to us the authority that Adam gave to the devil during his great fall. Do we surrender our will to our enemy during these waves of destruction? No!

So then, how are we the Church to respond?

Confession of Faith—I Will Not Be Silent!

Proclaiming and declaring the following confession of faith is an excellent response to the enemy's war plan:

In the name of Messiah, my Redeemer, with all boldness (Philemon 1:8), I will preach the Gospel (Mark 16:15), the Gospel of Peace (Romans 10:15), and I will speak the truth in love (Ephesians 4:15). I am ready in season and out of season to preach the Word, reprove, rebuke, and exhort (2 Timothy 4:2). I wisely decree a separation between spiritual light and darkness (Genesis 1:4). I prophesy life to dead bones (Ezekiel 37:4), and by faith I call things that are not as though they already were (Romans 4:17), and I live to declare the glory of the Lord (Psalm 118:17). I will worship Him in spirit and in truth (John 4:24), and speak to my brothers and sisters in the faith with psalms, hymns, and songs from the Spirit (Ephesians 5:19), all the days of my life (Psalm 23:6). I will not be silent (Psalm 30:12), amen and amen.

We Are Equipped with His Authority to Win

It's time to polish the shields, sharpen the swords, and tighten the belts, for the battle has begun. But we need not fear—we are equipped to win!

We have been given powerful spiritual weapons to win every battle that we face—including this one. To begin with, we have His authority over satan and all, not some, but all of his wicked works. Find your courage in Jesus' words to us in Luke 10:19 from the Amplified Version of the Bible: *"Listen carefully: I have given you authority [that you now possess] to tread on serpents and scorpions, and [the ability to exercise authority] over all the power of the enemy (Satan); and nothing will [in any way] harm you."*

We should not be controlled by fear, for God has given us the power of courage. Joshua 1:9 asks us, *"Have I not commanded you? Be strong and of good courage; do not be afraid, nor be dismayed, for the Lord your God is with you wherever you go."* Yes! With Almighty God on our side we have no reason to be bound up with fear.

In times like these we need to muster up courage and take down the power of the enemy around us. We need to walk in all boldness with the authority He gives to use to overcome all wickedness.

A Confession of Faith for Protection against Deadly Pestilence and Disease

Since our enemy continues to attack the people of this earth with deadly pestilence and disease, let's declare the following confession of faith for protection for ourselves and our families, and always in the name of Jehovah Rapha—our Healer.

In Your name, Jesus, I renounce the spirit of death and this (name of disease) that has come to steal, kill, and destroy us (John 10:10). And by the healing virtue of Your Holy Word, I apply the power of Your blood over myself and my family. I declare that no weapon formed against us will prosper (Isaiah 54:17), no evil will befall us, nor will any plague come near our dwelling (Psalm 91:10).

You, Lord, are faithful, who will establish us and guard us from the evil one (2 Thessalonians 3:3). But You also gave us Your authority to trample on serpents and scorpions, and over all the power of the enemy, and nothing shall by any means hurt us (Luke 10:19). You created us in Your image, as Jesus is, so are we on this earth. And You gave us dominion over every living thing that moves, including this disease (Genesis 1:26-28; 1 John 4:17).

Lord, You are our Refuge when we are oppressed, and in times of trouble. And we know Your name and we put our trust in You; for You, Lord, have not forsaken those who seek You (Psalm 9:9-10). I will bless my Lord, O my soul, and forget not all Your benefits: who forgives all our iniquities, who heals all our diseases (Psalm 103:2-3). And saves us from deadly pestilence (Psalm 91:3).

Willingly, You bore our griefs and carried our sorrows and pains, You were stricken, struck down and degraded and humiliated by the Father. You were wounded for our transgressions, crushed for our wickedness, [our sin, our injustice, and for our wrongdoing]; You were punished for our well-being, and by Your stripes (wounds) we are healed (see Isaiah 53:4-5 AMP).

Lord God, Your Word teaches us that death and life are in the power of the tongue, and those who love it and indulge it will eat its fruit and bear the consequences of their words (Proverbs 18:21). I surrender my tongue to You this day. I choose to speak life, not death over myself and family. I declare by faith that we will not die, but live and declare the works of the Lord (Psalm 118:17). And I declare that this disease will die in my hands; it cannot enter my body. And if it already made its way in there without my knowing, this disease dies and is eliminated from my body. I declare that every cell, tissue, organ, and system in my body are healed, made whole, strengthened, disease-free, and disease-proof for the glory of the Lord.

Lord God, I declare protection for the elderly and vulnerable members in my family. I stand on Your promise to give power to the weak; and to those who have no might, You increase strength (Isaiah 40:29). As we wait upon You, Lord, You shall renew our strength; we shall mount up with wings as eagles, we shall run and not be weary, and we shall walk and not faint (Isaiah 40:31).

I choose to believe Your report that promises to heal me and my loved ones in spirit, soul, and body (Isaiah 53:1,4-5). I will obey Your counsel and believe Your promise. I will not fear, for You are with me; I will not be dismayed, for You are my God. I believe You when You say to me that You will strengthen me. Yes, You will help me, You will uphold me with Your righteous right hand (Isaiah 41:10).

I will be still, and know that You are my God (Psalm 46:10), You will keep me in perfect peace because my mind is stayed on You and because I trust in You (Isaiah 26:3). The weapons of my warfare are not carnal but mighty in God for pulling down strongholds, casting down arguments and every high thing that exalts itself against the knowledge of God, bringing every thought into captivity to the obedience of Christ (2 Corinthians 10:4-5).

As for me and my house, we will serve the Lord (Joshua 24:15). Your Word is hidden in our hearts (Psalm 119:11); we will remain faithful and wise servants (Matthew 24:45-46); we choose Your joy for our strength (Nehemiah 8:10). We will love

You, Lord, with all our heart, soul, and mind, and we will love our neighbors as we love ourselves (Matthew 22:37-39). We will reach out to those in need and release Your healing power into those who are sick, because we believe they will be healed (Mark 16:17-18).

I encourage you to use this confession of faith against deadly pestilence and disease and pray it daily over yourself and your loved ones.

A Confession of Faith to Encourage Ourselves

I will not be dismayed or afraid this day (Joshua 1:9); I will take up my shield of faith (Ephesians 6:16) and the sword of the Spirit (Ephesians 6:17), and I will defeat my enemies— fear, intimidation, lack of confidence, even doubt and unbelief (Deuteronomy 28:7). No weapon formed against me will prosper (Isaiah 54:17). I have the Lord's authority (Luke 10:19). God is my avenger (Romans 12:19), and by His works I am worthy (Revelation 3:4). I am clothed with rich robes of forgiveness (Zechariah 3:4) and salvation (Isaiah 61:10). I am sober-minded and watchful (1 Peter 5:8) and I am strong in the Lord and in the strength of His might (Ephesians 6:10). I cannot be outwitted by satan (2 Corinthians 2:11). Nothing can separate me from the love of God (Romans 8:38-39). The devil has been defeated (Revelation 20:10).

The Battle Plan

By being passive and remaining silent, we got ourselves into this mess, and it will take the opposite action to get ourselves out of it. Look at this portion of Scripture in Second Chronicles 7:14:

If My people who are called by My name will humble themselves, and pray and seek My face, and turn from their wicked ways, then will I hear from heaven, and will forgive their sin and heal their land.

I believe the humbling process within the true Church has already begun. We know we can't run the true ministry with our own strength—we must rely upon His strength and His strength alone. Proverbs 3:5-6 tells us, *"Trust in the Lord with all your heart, and lean not on your own understanding; in all your ways acknowledge Him, and He shall direct your paths."*

We are to pray. If you are a pastor of a local church, I suggest you gather up people to pray around the clock 24/7. And may God's house return to His original plan—a House of Prayer. Jesus says in Mark 11:17, *"...Is it not written, 'My house shall be called a house of prayer for all nations'?..."* Gather the people in and pray around the clock until this wickedness is broken off us. First Thessalonians 5:17 simply says, *"Pray without ceasing."* When we are corporately united together it will be easier for us to accomplish.

We are to seek God's face. And what does it mean to seek His face? It means to seek His presence. The Scriptures tell us in First Chronicles 22:19, *"Now set your heart and your soul to seek the Lord your God...."* This is a personal journey to seek the Lord with our heart, mind, and emotions—to seek the will of the Father in all situations. And we can take our personal journey and link it with others during this time and empower the cause to take back what the enemy has stolen from us. Deuteronomy 32:30 talks about how one can chase a thousand, and two can put ten thousand to flight. If we have a massive prayer effort, we can break through the power of the enemy rising against us.

In addition to around-the-clock intercession, we must repent of our sins. Without true repentance, we will not overcome the enemy in this battle. We have to be honest with ourselves and admit our sins and ask the Lord to forgive us, and then we must turn away from wickedness. Acts 3:19 reveals the end result of repentance, *"Repent therefore and be converted, that your sins may be blotted out, so that times of refreshing may come from the presence of the Lord."*

If we activate our faith, pray, seek, and repent, God promises us to heal our land. And we need our land to heal. The Church can no longer remain silent. We must be willing to risk it all to regain what the enemy has stolen from us.

Prayer

Father God, You know our plight. We turn to You and acknowledge that we can't undo this in the power of our own strength, but only by the power of Your might. We choose this day to repent from all unrighteous, to turn from our wicked ways, and seek Your face daily. We humbly ask for Your forgiveness for our passiveness, and we ask for Your strength to do all that is necessary to turn this situation around and regain our freedom to worship You freely again. In Jesus' name, we pray, amen.

We have discussed throughout this chapter that we as the Church must not remain silent and have honestly addressed issues why many of God's people are being passive and silent about things they should be passionate and openly speaking out about. In the next chapter we focus on surrendering our weakness and our strength to God in this most important hour.

Faith Assignment

If you are a member of a local church, go to your pastor and ask if you can organize a prayer group for the nation as discussed in this chapter. If you belong to a small group, talk about ways you can gather people together to pray for the Church worldwide and for our nation to repent. Even if it is you by yourself, begin to pray daily for the Church and for our nation to repent.

Questions to Ponder and Answer for Chapter 9: We Cannot Remain Silent

1. What would make it a lot easier for the devil to do his dirty business?

    _____

    _____

    _____

2. What can silence the Church if we let it?

    _____

    _____

    _____

3. What's the main reason the Church is silent?

    _____

    _____

    _____

4. Matthew 6:24 talks about two masters, and that we either serve one or the other. Who and what are the two masters?

    _____

    _____

    _____

5. The devil's army is trying to steal what?

    _____

    _____

    _____

6. According to Luke 10:19, what have you been given?

_____

_____

_____

7. What Scripture reveals God's plan to heal our land?

_____

_____

_____

Personal Assessment

Have I been silent? If so why? Am I afraid of what others might think about me? Am I afraid of losing my job? Am I willing to use my voice and share with others what the Lord puts on my heart to speak about? Are there topics very near to my heart that I believe I need to speak about with those around me? If so, what are these topics?

Group Discussion

As a group, talk about why the Church has been silent during these pressing times of persecution against the Church. How might you begin to open up and share with others about what the Bible has to say about some of these pressing matters plaguing society and the Church today. Ask the group to come up with a list of 3-5 topics that they believe are of most importance to begin to speak up about.

10

Surrendering Our Weakness and Strength to Him

Word of the Lord

The Spirit of the Living God would say to you this day,

> Hand it over, give it to Me and when you do I can set you free. Be free from the power of the weakness that taunts you with thoughts of never measuring up to My standard. It is I in you who causes My Spirit to move freely through you. It is never the power of your strength that accomplishes great glories in this day. Humble yourself before Me so that I can set you free from pride and arrogance. And in doing so, I am free to move through you. Trust Me and lean not on your own understanding in all of this.

I say to you this day.

As odd as it may seem, we need to come to a point where we are willing to surrender and hand over our strength to God. This act is often the breaking point for our breakthrough that releases our manifested miracle.

Our Strength Can Become a Hindrance

One of the most difficult tasks in our personal walk with our Lord is to surrender our strength to Him. Psalm 20:7 (AMP) tells us, *"Some trust in chariots and some in horses, but we will remember and trust in the name of the Lord our God."* When I read this portion of Scripture, I understand "chariots" to be the latest in this world's technology, and I see "horses" represent human speed and strength. We can get ourselves into so much trouble when we put our trust in these human means instead of relying upon God's wisdom and strength.

It seems easier for us to accept the counsel that we are to surrender our weaknesses to God than our strengths. After all, we've been taught that our weaknesses are faults. And it is true we are to give our weaknesses to God, but our strengths can also be hindrances.

Surrender Our Weakness to Him

Let's look to our weaknesses first. All too often we have the misconception that God uses only very gifted people to do great tasks for Him. But as we read through our Bibles we find that this is not always the case. It is actually God's greatness within us that enables us to do anything at all. But we fight God in this and want to hold on to this sacred cow that it is our strength that accomplishes the miraculous moves of the Spirit of God.

Let's take a brief look into the life of Moses to bring this viewpoint into a clearer focus. Please read through Exodus 6:28 to 7:13.

Now, that you've read through this portion of Scripture, let's talk about it.

God calls Moses to be a spokesperson, a prophet for Him, and tells him that he is to go before the Pharaoh and tell him all that He instructs him to say. But Moses, being afraid of his weakness (a speech problem), uses it as an excuse to try to bow out of his calling from God.

And let's face it, we can be just as guilty as Moses in this area. We are so accustomed to believing the negative perspective of the world about ourselves that it blurs our vision to see God's ability working through us. But when we break free from this identity crisis, we can surrender to

God's will to use common and ordinary people like us for His glory. I believe we can agree that God moved mightily through the weakness of Moses for His great glory! And He will do the same for us as well.

Consequences of Moral Weakness

And may I be perfectly clear here, I am not talking about moral weaknesses such as pornography, unfaithfulness, and the like. Refusal to repent will stop the flow of God's anointing in our lives until true repentance comes; even though we repent of sin doesn't mean we will not reap the consequences of those sins. Look at the life of King David and his adulterous affair with another man's wife, Bathsheba. She became pregnant, and to try to hide his sin, David plotted her husband Uriah's death. He dies on the frontlines of a battle, and David takes Bathsheba as his wife, and thinks all is well hidden. Because there is no repentance, God sends prophet Nathaniel to rebuke. At this point King David confesses his wrongdoings and his life is spared, but it did not prevent him from bearing the consequence of his hidden sins of lust, adultery, lying and murder. The son who was conceived during David and Bathsheba's act of adultery dies.

And even though he fulfills his destiny, he bore the deep battle scars of his moral weakness.

Please read this powerful lesson about the consequences of moral weakness from King David's life in Second Samuel 11-12.

Blanche Surrenders Her Weakness

My friend and intercessor, Blanche, shares with us a time in her life that she too surrendered her strength to God. She shares, "I was brought up in a large family that went to church every Sunday and followed its teachings. I was sent to a religious school from grade 1-12. With this atmosphere, I was introduced to God which started the seed of impartation of the life of God in me to grow spiritually."

My father enforced strict obedience to authority at the expense of allowing my personal freedom. Amid a difficult childhood, I learned that I could not rely on my own strength, but I had to turn to Jesus to find my unconditional love, peace, and joy. I remember when I was seven, I had experienced a new feeling of holiness; I could come to Him when I did wrong and asked forgiveness. I wanted to be devoted to God. When I look back, this was the time I really had been reborn, changed from above, although I never remember not being without God.

I was not a particularly good student in grade school and was pressured to get good grades because that mattered. I was even called "dummy" by my dad. I did not like that, so I cheated on tests to get passing grades. When I was in third grade, I knew I was doing wrong and became convicted of my sin. I remember deciding to not cheat and suffer the consequences of failing. Somehow God would help me. My father was furious with my extremely poor grades. That year I failed third grade and had to go to summer school. I was humiliated but I knew I had done the right thing not to offend God. After summer school I was passed on to fourth grade. For several years I had to ask God to help me not to start cheating again. God gave me the strength to try harder and to do the right thing. I had to trust God to save me from this sin.

Every year I would ask him to join a daddy-daughter club at my school, but he always refused. In eleventh grade I heard the Lord tell me to pay for the club's dues with the money I made cleaning houses and not to tell anyone and so I did. In the middle of eleventh grade my father was diagnosed with cancer and in the summer died. I and my mother found out the following school year that because my dad and I were in the daddy/daughter club, my tuition would be paid for in my senior year. Glory to God! My God took care of me. I was sad about my father's passing but felt relieved from my dad's authoritarian power. I leaned into God and wanted more of Him. I heard about the baptism in the Holy Spirit and asked God to receive the baptism because I wanted more of Him. I got what I asked for. I immediately was baptized in the Holy Spirit with evidence of speaking in tongues. Now I started to believe God even more.

After high school I went to a community college, walked in faith that God would lead me as to what to do with my life. I finished the first two years with all grades of A's and B's. I went on to a university and graduated with honors. I realized I had been living and believing a lie. I was not irrelevant or dumb. I went on to graduate school and graduated with high honors. Glory to God!

After college I became a special education teacher. I found that when I asked the Lord how to teach my students who had special individual differences, He told me how. I had a strong compassion and understanding of feeling different and needing a coach to help them achieve a higher level of personal success in life. I would go to the Lord asking Him to show me what to do. He gave me specific techniques to break down learning activities so they could understand and feel successful, and they did succeed. I saw how I was prepared to work with students needing an aided education and I got great joy in doing so. All praise to God!

My experiences with God that brought me to a deeper level in Him as an adult have always taken place as I had an inner hunger and thirst for more of Him. As an adult I learned that my strength comes from God when I totally surrender to Him. By honoring, praising, and worshipping God, I discovered He IS the great "I Am"; a God who is faithful and more than enough. All that mattered was to keep my eyes on Him, repent when I made a mistake, ask to be washed in the blood of Jesus to be made whole and continue to build an intimate relationship with Him. When I surrendered myself totally in life's challenges and believed He cared about me, I was able to walk in faith. When the enemy comes to feed me lies, I take authority and cast those thoughts down in the name of Jesus, so I do not give any thought to his lies. I tell satan to leave in Jesus' name. I do not accept his thoughts. I rebuke him and find a Scripture promise (the opposite of what he suggested) and meditate on God's Word and let God minister to me.

I found I had to come to Father God, as a child, asking Him for help. I did not have the answers to my life, He did. I needed Holy Spirit's help. When I became quiet before Him and yielded to Him, I encountered the presence of God and the power to overcome. I became bold in my ways. God has been so faithful to me as I submitted my ways for His. I became new. I learned that God really is so close, He is within me. I am His forever!

Surrender Our Strength to God

Let's now turn our attention to the act of surrendering our strength to God, for this too can become a great hindrance that prevents the supernatural will and acts of our Messiah from coming forth in our lives.

As stated earlier, one of the most difficult things in our walk with God can be to surrender our strength to Him. Why would this be? A few reasons could be that we have to humble ourselves before God.

We have to admit that we are prideful and we forget that it's His greatness in us that causes the miraculous intervention of God to manifest in our lives.

Let's look at the life of Samson and all of his strength. We can read about the life of Samson in Judges 13-16. Please read this portion of Scripture now and then we will talk a little bit about his life.

An angel of the Lord visited Samson's barren mother and told her that she would have a son and that God had a special plan for him. He was called to be a Nazarite, a calling that had a restricted lifestyle regarding what he could and could not eat or drink, along with specific rules such as not cutting his hair or going near a dead body. Along with the restrictions of being called to live the lifestyle of a Nazarite, Samson was empowered with supernatural strength from God. Even though people are called by God does not mean they will obey His calling or His commands. Samson was constantly pushing the limits with God. He did not make the connection that his strength came from God, and foolishly wasted his God-given strength.

He's not much different from many of God's servants today. We are too quick to forget that our gifts and talents, our wisdom and strength are not humanly conceived, but God-given. And because of this willful forgetfulness, we never quite surrender as we ought to, and we limit God's full power within us. Our strength can actually become a hindrance and prevent the things we desire the most from manifesting in our lives.

Surrendering Her Human Strength

One of the most powerful moments during my many years in the healing ministry happened in Purcellville, Virginia, in May 2019. Now I remind you I have seen a lot. I have many precious moments in ministry, and each one touches my spirit in different ways and pulls on the power of God activated within me.

I had been teaching the people all day at an annual healing conference about how to believe and receive their supernatural healing, and then that evening I released this healing power into the people. Many miracles were taking place, but something touched the center of my heart so deeply that it released something within me and the tsunami wave of healing glory was loosed.

A woman was standing at the altar with her hands held out in front of her surrendering her human strength to God. Do you know what was in her hands? A set of hearing aids. And as it says in Psalm 20:7, *"Some trust in chariots and some in horses, but we will remember and trust in the name of the Lord our God."* The hearing aids she was giving up to her Lord and Healer were her chariots and horses. Remember in the beginning of this chapter I told you what these things represent? Chariots represent the latest in this world's technology, and horses represent human speed and strength.

In this act of bravery, she was admitting before her God that she had been trusting in the world's wisdom and strength, and she no longer wanted to have this in her spiritual resume. She was willing to hand over her human strength and tap into His supernatural healing power. And as she did, I kid you not, when I placed healing hands upon her, not only were her ears opened, but the rest of the people after her in that particular line were instantly healed.

Surrendering our human strength to God Almighty plows down the roadblocks standing between us and our manifested miracles.

Now let us look at surrendering our strength to God.

The Positive Side of God-Given Strength

Strength is not all bad—only the strength that is not surrendered to God and hinders us from fulfilling what the Lord has for us to do, and to do in His way.

Let's quickly look at the life of Caleb in the Bible. When God rescued the Israelites from the pharaoh's wicked trade of slavery, He led His people into the wilderness with the promise to bring them into the Promised Land. He made great promises to them about their new way of life in their new land. During their journey, God provided for their every need, and yet the people whined and complained against Moses.

Then Moses sent out twelve young men to spy out the land of Canaan for him. Ten out of the twelve spies returned with a negative and hopeless report, except Caleb and Joshua. And this is where the God-given strength of faith comes into play.

We, like the negative spies, can magnify problems we face, or we can glorify the power of the Lord's provision. What are we going to lift up in our lives? The strength of doubt and unbelief? Or the strength of faith? Caleb and Joshua chose the strength of faith and returned with a favorable report about the land of Canaan.

Perhaps you have received the promise of God in His Word to heal you, but you have spied out the situation and like the negative spies have been overcome by fear, doubt, and unbelief because you have been focusing on the wrong thing—the plague. But God continues to speak throughout His Word healing promises that minister to your mind and emotions. What are you going to do? Will you continue to report the troubles facing you, or will you make the changes necessary and surrender that weakness of fear, doubt, and unbelief to the Lord? It's the only way to walk into the promised land of healing.

Remember the lady earlier in this chapter who surrendered her strength, the hearing aids, to the Lord, and her weakness, fear, doubt and unbelief to Him as well—when she did, her long-awaited miracle manifested.

How about you? What do you need to surrender? What strength in your life is hindering your promise to manifest? And what weaknesses are standing in the way? Are you willing to let go of these hindrances and allow God's miracle-working power to flow through your spirit, soul, and body?

Prayer

As the psalmist prays in Psalm 139:23-24 (NIV), I lift up this same prayer to You, Oh Lord, "Search me, God, and know my heart; test me and know my anxious thoughts. See if there is any offensive way in me, and lead me in the way everlasting." In the name of the Father, Son Jesus Christ, and Holy Spirit, I pray and wait on You to answer, amen and amen.

In this chapter we have seen how the negative thoughts and actions of others against us can become a weakness in our life and a roadblock to fulfilling our God-given destiny when we adopt them as truth. We have also come to the realization that often our strength becomes the weak link that prevents our manifested miracles from coming forth. But the moment we surrender this strength of ours over to God, the healing comes forth. In the next chapter we find out how Holy Spirit wills to personally train ordinary people like us to do extraordinary things for Him in these last days.

Faith Assignment

This chapter's faith assignment is to examine your heart and be brutally honest with yourself. What do you personally feel are your weaknesses? Write them down. And be just as honest and write down what you believe to be your strengths. Take this list before the Lord in prayer and ask Him to speak to your heart as to whether or not these weaknesses and strengths have become actual hindrances in your personal walk and calling with God.

Questions to Ponder and Answer for Chapter 10: Surrendering Our Weakness and Strength to Him

1. What act is often the breaking point for your breakthrough that releases your manifested miracle?

   _____

   _____

   _____

2. What does Psalm 20:7 (AMP) say?

   _____

   _____

   _____

3. What might be the meaning of "chariots"?

   _____

   _____

   _____

4. And what do "horses" represent in Psalm 20:7?

   _____

   _____

   _____

5. Do you have a misconception about who God uses?

   _____

   _____

   _____

6. What allows you to be able to do anything at all for God?

    _____

    _____

    _____

7. Refusal to repent will stop what in your life?

    _____

    _____

    _____

8. What are a few reasons why it may be difficult for you to surrender your strength to God?

    _____

    _____

    _____

9. What are you too quick to forget about?

    _____

    _____

    _____

10. How can you be like the ten negative spies?

    _____

    _____

    _____

11. Instead of being like the spies with the negative report, you can be like Caleb and Joshua and do what?

    _____

Personal Assessment

The message of this chapter has caused me to stop and examine my heart. Have I entered into pride and because of it my cherished answers to my prayers are being hindered as a result of pride? Have I been quick to forget that my gifts and talents, wisdom and strength are not humanly conceived, but God-given? Or am I the opposite and do not see myself as God sees me and my low self-esteem is preventing the workings of God's ability within me? What am I going to do about this?

Group Discussion

Most every believer desires to be pleasing to our heavenly Father, but are we allowing God to be who He is within us? Or are there hindrances standing in the way of Him moving freely in our lives? Can we come up with several examples of how our weaknesses and strengths can stand in the way of what God truly has planned for us?

11

The Church Is Breaking Out!

Word of the Lord

The Spirit of the Living God would say to you this day,

> Dead bones must rise again! Shake off the sleep and the slumber. Press toward the mark of your high calling. Unleash the resurrection power of My Spirit within you. No longer be timid and shy. You have entered into a time when there is no turning back for My Beloved—My Church.
>
> I have empowered you for this time, this day, and for this moment. No longer will you remain silent as the world passes away. I have given you a voice; it is time to lift it up and use it for My glory.
>
> Reject the lukewarm waters that are trying to consume you. Refresh yourself with the coolness of My Spirit. And as you quickly refresh, for the time is ever so short, allow the Living Water within you to heat up until it boils over to all those around you. You have no time to lap in the vomit of passiveness.
>
> That same Spirit that raised Me, the Living Christ, from the dead lives within you and is warming up the dead bones— and as you surrender to this life-giving power of Mine, those dead bones will come back to life again.

I am the One whom you want to reach out and touch. And as you do—I will be there to meet you with all power in this last hour. It is time for My people who are called by My name to rise up in the power of My might.

And what is My name? I Am the Great I Am. I Am the Messiah—the One True Savior of this world. I bled and died for you, because of My great passion for you. You are created in My image, and I am passionate about My Father. And I am passionate for My Beloved Bride—the Church. And you are created to be passionate about Me and My Father.

Although the attacks are strong, My Spirit within you is even stronger. Rise up! Leave that fear behind you. Take courage in knowing that you do not fight this battle alone, for I fight for you. This battle belongs to Me, and you are My mighty warrior destined to conquer, not be conquered.

I call forth the dead bones within the Body to rise up with My power as your strength. I call forth a refreshing to the new person within you. I command you to forsake the past, no longer look back with longing for what once was, but stand for hope of My soon return.

Be not afraid in these last days, but be strong and courageous. Know that your faith is your shield. And My Word is your sword. The end is predetermined—and you are created to win.

All creation is ready, and the heavens and the earth are beckoning Me to raise up the Church in this great hour. I have created you to release My power among the lost inhabitants of this earth. For it is passing away, and it must for My new Heaven and new earth to manifest. Release the Kingdom of God on this earth. It's time; position yourself with My Spirit.

> All hell is about to break out. You think, "It's time to run and hide." And I say, "No! It's not time to run and hide—it's time for My Beloved Bride—My Church to allow My resurrection power of life to cause those dead bones to arise."
>
> Surrender your spirit, soul, and body onto Me—allow Me to fight through you.

Thus says the Alpha and the Omega, the Beginning and the End.

The Resurgence of Resurrection Power

One of the main ingredients in this tsunami wave of healing glory is the resurgence of the resurrection power of our risen Lord in us. We've had this power of the resurrection since the moment we were rebirthed in the Spirit—the day we were born again, but we allowed it to be dormant within us, but the everlasting Father says, *"It's time for us to activate the supernatural resurrection power in us."* For there is a great battle between the Spirit of Life and the spirit of death.

Let's obey the Father's words to us and activate the supernatural resurrection power in us. Read this amazing prophecy from Ezekiel 37:4-14:

Again He said to me, "Prophesy to these bones, and say to them, 'O dry bones, hear the word of the Lord! Thus says the Lord God to these bones: "Surely I will cause breath to enter into you, and you shall live. I will put sinews on you and bring flesh upon you, cover you with skin and put breath in you; and you shall live. Then you shall know that I am the Lord.""

So I prophesied as I was commanded; and as I prophesied, there was a noise, and suddenly a rattling; and the bones came together, bone to bone. Indeed, as I looked, the sinews and the flesh came upon them, and the skin covered them over; but there was no breath in them.

Also He said to me, "Prophesy to the breath, prophesy, son of man, and say to the breath, 'Thus says the Lord God: "Come from the four winds, O breath, and breathe on these slain, that they may live."'" So I prophesied as He commanded me, and breath came into them, and they lived, and stood upon their feet, an exceedingly great army.

Then He said to me, "Son of man, these bones are the whole house of Israel. They indeed say, 'Our bones are dry, our hope is lost, and we ourselves are cut off!' Therefore prophesy and say to them, 'Thus says the Lord God: "Behold, O My people, I will open your graves and cause you to come up from your graves, and bring you into the land of Israel. Then you shall know that I am the Lord, when I have opened your graves, O My people, and brought you up from your graves. I will put My Spirit in you, and you shall live, and I will place you in your own land. Then you shall know that I, the Lord, have spoken it and performed it," says the Lord.'"

Because the Lord tells us in Matthew 9:38, *"Therefore pray the Lord of the harvest to send out laborers into His harvest,"* I challenge us to release a mighty move of Holy Spirit and harvest a multitude of lost people inside the dead Church. And before you get all excited and close the book, hear me out. Some people believe that God exists, but they have been indoctrinated with a spirit of religion and haven't seen the truth about being relational with Him. I believe there is a harvest to be picked within the Church. And they in turn will become workers for God in this great harvest.

With this great loss of so many within the establishment of the Church to a spirit of religion and to the ways of the world, let us love as the Father loves, and release the resurrection power of life as the priest and prophet Ezekiel did during the darkest days of Judah. Let's repurpose this prophecy and release the dead bones within the Church today to become living, breathing evangelists who proclaim worldwide the Good News of Jesus Christ.

Let's begin to prophetically pray and use the power of life and death in our words (see Proverbs 18:21).

We pray,

> *Spirit of the Living God breathe upon the religious with fresh breath that many may revive and come alive in the Spirit. We create with words of faith spiritual sinews and declare vitality and strength into the very fiber of Your Church.*

We release a blessing of Holy Spirit revival over churches that the glory of the Lord may cover lost souls like the flesh upon their mortal bodies.

> *We proclaim directly to you, Church, that you will not remain in a state of death, but that you repent and give your lives over to the true saving grace of our Lord Jesus Christ. Receive the breath of the Living God and come alive, be born from above, and become all that you are meant to become in these last days.*
>
> *We prophetically hear by faith, and rejoice for you as we can hear a rattling noise of your bones coming together. We see within you and see your sinews, and see the God flesh, the new self grow. We see the skin of His glory cover you and feel the first breaths of His resurrection life rebirth within you.*
>
> *We declare by faith you once were dead, but now you live and have your being in Him. We release you into this great harvest field—fulfill the destiny that you are called to and win the lost for the glory of the Lord, amen.*

A Fast and Furious Wave

Fast and furious is the fifth wave of the tsunami wave of healing glory encompassing this entire earth. I have witnessed this wave time and time again during healing conferences, seminars, and special healing services. Where Holy Spirit has released the wave of worship that softens the hard-heartedness of the people, then comes a strong wave of repentance, then washes in a wave of revelation truth that sets the people free from doubt and unbelief.

Then sweeps in a fresh anointing of the baptism of Holy Spirit with the evidence of the people praying in their supernatural languages. Next comes in this fast and furious wave of God Almighty against a spirit of death that has tried to drown the people of God. And this is where I witness the vengeance of the Lord rise against satan and his wicked works with a force that is unexplainable. God cherishes His people. And this war between our Redeemer and the devil is a fierce battle.

When we willingly step out of the way and allow God to be almighty in our physical bodies, the enemy doesn't stand a chance against the Spirit of the Living God in us.

I was ministering in Sweden recently, and the healing line was especially long one night. I came upon one woman who was bound to a wheelchair. But a fast and furious wave of healing was released and instantly she was healed and walked. Her husband pushed the wheelchair out the door after the meeting while she walked out in her own strength.

Word of the Lord

The Spirit of the Lord would say to you this day:

> It's time to rise and shine with the resurrection power of Holy Spirit.

It's time to rise and shine with all boldness, not withholding in this late hour.

It's time to rise and shine and declare the goodness of God to a lost and dying world.

Yes, the antichrist spirit is rising up quickly, and it's strong—but even still, greater am I, Jesus, in you then he, satan, who is in this world.

I created you to be a light in the darkness; now rise and shine, and yes, give God the glory.

I created you to be victorious, now fight the good fight of faith.

I created you to be a conqueror—more than a conqueror.

But you cannot win if you will not fight the battle before you.

Pick up your spiritual weapons and fight the way My Word instructs you.

In Me you are undefeated.

With Me you win.

And I created you to win always, not just once in a while.

But you choose this day to win or to give up.

Remember, I never gave up on you and I never will.

I overcame the human will so you can overcome it too.

This is the first step to win any and every battle that you face.

Now remember to rise and shine with My resurrection power today.

And again I say, "My beloved, it's time to rise and shine."

An Unstoppable Wave of Healing Glory

Now we examine the sixth wave, the most powerful wave of healing glory that cannot be stopped. It rushes through people with a great healing force. This is the wave that will reach the masses in these latter times, whether they are in large gatherings or one-on-one times of ministry. It will take everyone who is willing and obedient to the calling of God to win the lost. Although the devil hates us, he can never separate us from this wonderful wave of healing glory. This wave is fed by the pure and undefiled love of God—and it's unstoppable.

All the other waves in this supernatural tsunami have been building up for such a time as this according to God's timeline. While the birth pangs are one on top of another and all hell is breaking loose against every person alive today—so too God's heavenly Kingdom with great and unlimited power is invading the earth like never before.

I am telling you that this end times wave of healing glory has hit the shores of the Western world. A mighty wave of healing power is moving quickly throughout the entire earth, including the West. As I minister throughout the earth, I am witnessing a surge of the power of the Holy Spirit being released in greater measure and it is ever increasing over His people.

I shared with you a few pages back about the fast and furious wave and how the woman in Sweden was instantly delivered and healed from that wheelchair. Well, that fast and furious wave launched the unstoppable wave of healing glory and many people were instantly healed of many types of infirmities.

Next to her was a woman suffering from fibromyalgia. She too was instantly released from the power of this disease and rejoiced for God's mercy. A sudden and unstoppable wave of healing glory broke forth and the long lines of people suffering from many different aliments were quickly delivered and healed from such things as deafness and injuries of the spine, neck, and shoulders. People were jumping up and down as their knees and feet were instantly healed.

There is so much healing power being released in this tsunami wave of healing glory that I have started to minister to people in groups according to the disease. For example, deafness. Whether the people are suffering from complete or partial deafness, in one ear or both ears, I ask them to stand together in a line and I minister to the entire group, like I would with one person.

I renounce the spirit of deafness, I release the Spirit of Life into their ears, and prophetically command that their ears be recreated, realigned, and are healed and made whole. As we activate our faith, they all close their eyes, I shut off the mics, and I walk farther and farther away, asking them if they can hear me. And they do.

Whatever your need is, trust God, and expect to get healed with His amazing healing power of glory during these last days.

How Do We Reach the Multitudes?

You might be wondering how do we reach the multitudes during this time of chaos. I have to agree that with the level of lawlessness ramping up so quickly around us, there are moments that this task set before us seems insurmountable. In these moments I have to force every thought captive and fix my eyes on the Good Shepherd and follow His loving lead into the valley of the lost. I have a place specially designed by God—my arena of influence—and I am called by Him to reach specific people.

You too have an arena of influence that Elohim has predestined just for you—a group of people who will hear the message you have to share and receive the love of the Father that you have to give them. And they will receive the gift of grace that has been worked within you for such a time as this. By living out our calling in our arena of influence, everyone has the opportunity they need to hear the Good News of salvation.

The Church Is Breaking Out!

I love the fact that the Church, the true followers of the Victorious One are breaking out of the four walls of our gathering places. The Body of Christ is stepping up to the plate and going out to the people as we should be, especially during these trying times.

For some of us this comes easier as we have been going about our heavenly Father's business for a long time. While for others it is new territory and they need a little encouragement and guidance. So let's discuss how to "break out."

God Uses Ordinary People

So many of God's people have the misconception that they can't be used by God because they didn't attend a Bible school. This is so far from the truth. God is not seeking out people with titles, seminary degrees, or extensive ministry experience. That's not how God operates.

When we read through the Bible we see that God chooses ordinary people to do His will. We read in Acts 4:13 just how ordinary these men were: *"Now when they saw the boldness of Peter and John, and perceived that they were uneducated and untrained men, they marveled. And they realized that they had been with Jesus."*

It's not a coincidence that the fact that Peter and John were uneducated and untrained men is recorded for all to see. These words were penned by the inspiration of Holy Spirit for us today. And the Chief Cornerstone makes this point for us to grasp on to the type of individual God chooses, which goes against the worldly way of promoting. It also removes our poor excuses about not doing what God calls us to do in this late hour. And what is this excuse? "I have no formal biblical training so I can't be used by God."

As we read about the apostles, we can clearly see that they did not have theological training before they were called by the Messiah to come and follow Him. These men were ordinary, everyday type of people. The known professions among this group were fishermen, business owners, a tax collector, and a zealot (a politician or revolutionary). Again, there was no formal religious education recorded in their background.

They were normal people with everyday needs just like you and me. As the Lord did not require titles, seminary degrees, or extensive ministry experience from them—He does not require these things from us either to serve Him.

Willing Hearts

We've established the fact that Peter and John were common, everyday fishermen, and yet they are among the twelve disciples chosen by the Messiah to join His team to change the world, and that they did. Although they were not the most intellectual or the wealthiest in the community, what they did have going for them was that they were willing to follow after Him. And they were quick to do so. Another quality I believe is often overlooked is that Peter and John were quick to recognize true greatness when they encountered it. And were compelled to follow after Him.

Are you among the common people of this earth? Do you recognize the greatness of God in our Lord? Are you compelled to follow after Him? And more importantly, is your heart willing to do as He asks of you? It's this willingness of a heart surrendered to Him that qualifies you to be used of the Lord in these latter times.

I have inclined my heart to perform Your statutes forever, to the very end (Psalm 119:112).

Holy Spirit Will Train You

If you will be like Peter and John and the other disciples and join the Messiah's team in these last days, He will personally train you. His type of training is hands-on and teaches you while on the job. You read in the Word that if you believe, you will lay hands on the sick and they will recover (see Mark 16:18). He then sends you out to the infirmed and has you do what you read in His Word, the Holy Bible. This is the method the Lord trained me, and it is very effective.

My training was intense, sometimes scary, and other times exciting, and it was always outside of my comfort zone. It was personal, one-on-one, and fully orchestrated by Holy Spirit Himself. With a willing heart, I chose to follow after Him and His ways. I read the Word that if I believed, I would cast out demons. Guess what came my way? Demon-possessed people. So I followed my Lord Jesus' example from the Holy Bible and cast them out everywhere I went. The Lord sent them to me—even to come and live under our roof as well, in the children's home. This on-the-job training was intense in every sense of the Word, but the Lord taught me to confront demons head-on, not to fear them, and how to overcome them.

I studied and actually fasted on the life teachings of our Redeemer. I learned that I was created in His image and that as He is, so am I on this earth. He is anointed, so I am now anointed. He released the gift of sight to the blind, so I knew I was empowered to do the same. Then the people who needed this great gift of sight began to come my way; sure it was stepping out of my comfort zone, especially in the beginning. But one thing I know is, I do not walk this earth alone—my Lord is with me every step of the way. And I began to witness blind eyes see, which are precious moments embedded in my memory.

To recap the seven key points of His hands-on training:

1. With a willing heart I choose to follow after Him and His ways.
2. I study the Holy Bible.
3. I fast on His teachings.
4. I believe His Word as undeniable truth.
5. I step out of my comfort zone.

6. The Lord either brings me to the infirmed or they come to me for ministry.

7. I follow His example recorded in the Scriptures and see results.

The same can happen with you. You believe God's Word is undeniably true, so you begin to lay hands on the sick around you. As you grow in this truth, you begin to see the infirmed around you healed and made whole.

Through my books, recorded messages, seminars, and conferences, I have been training people around the world throughout the years, and many of my readers are activating their faith and ministering healing to others. The following is one such testimony from Paulette who has been standing in faith for herself and others for deliverance and healing from cancer.

She writes, "Thank you for continuous prayer and mentorship in the Word of God. I am thankful to the Lord for the books you have written. It's like the words of the book are ministering to me and strengthening my faith.

"Jesus is the Healer; early in the morning I read the Healing Creed and praying for others who are sick. I heard a voice say to me, 'I am going before you.' I had a follow-up doctor appointment that morning and boldness welled up inside me.

"I have been praying for my colleague Debbie, and encouraging her with the Word of God through your books on healing. Debbie shared with me she had to take a CT scan to see if the tumors and cancer were leaving her body. I have never done this before but this boldness came over me to agree in prayer right then with her for healing, regardless if we were in front of the doctor office. Right there we agreed in prayer for her healing.

"Hallelujah! Debbie called later and shared she received her test results and the tumors had all shrunk in size.

"And during that same day my blood work came back looking so good that my doctor wrote a letter to my place of employment clearing me back to work at full capacity and doing well. My doctor said I only need to continue with routine check-ups. I will continue to speak the healing Scriptures over my body.

"At the cancer center, I have been witnessing to others and sharing your books, *The Healing Creed* and *The Prophetic and Healing Power of Your Words* to medical staff. They are hungry to learn about the Jesus the Healer. Thank you for mentoring me to continue to pray for others."

God's Qualifications for His Servants

The point has been made very clear that God uses ordinary people just like you and me to do His bidding on earth. Now just what are the qualities our Lord looks for in His servants? Second Chronicles 16:9 tells us that, *"the eyes of the Lord run to and fro throughout the whole earth, to show Himself strong on behalf of those whose heart is loyal to Him...."*

God is looking for people who have a loyal heart for Him. In other words, He is looking for individuals who are sold out for Jesus. The people who remember their first love, their Savior, and who are faithful, honorable, humble, and truthful to Him.

What I have learned through this Scripture is that we are the deciding factor as to whether or not God will use us. It's not about talents and abilities, it's about your spiritual heart condition toward Him. And the good news with this is, if you don't like the condition of your heart toward Him, you can do something about it—repent and make the necessary changes to be sold out for your Messiah in the troubling days ahead of us.

Having the Time of His Life Doing God's Business

Whatever you do from here on out, be about God's business. Activate the supernatural power of Holy Spirit in everything you do, and walk in all boldness in destressing times and good times as well.

I received the following beautiful letter from a 77-year-old man named Bill. He writes, "I bought your book, *The Prophetic & Healing Power of Your Words,* and have read it about five times. It has definitely changed my life and ministry. In the last two years we have seen God heal at least 40 people, mostly from small aches and pains. And I am now making house calls for people suffering with cancer."

Bill continues, "I have been saved since 1973, and filled with the Holy Spirit. I teach and train the Body of Christ for the work of the ministry. I witness out in the streets and shopping malls, and then I offer to pray for the sick. And I am having the time of my life serving the Lord."

Can you imagine the glory that would burst out around us if we all would do as Bill is doing, taking this healing message and making house calls in the name of the Lord? Do you know of sick individuals who need a healing touch from God? Be about your heavenly Father's business and pay them a visit today.

Prayer

Dear Holy Spirit, I long to be used in these last days for Your glory according to Your will. Help me overcome a religious spirit and the ways of this world. Even though I may seem ordinary, I know now that I am the kind of person You long to work through. So I invite You into my life; teach and train me to humble myself to You. In Your most precious holy name, amen.

Faith Assignment

This chapter's faith assignment has to do with breaking out of your comfort zone for the Lord. Do you feel all nervous inside about laying hands on the sick and ministering healing to them in the name of the Lord? Or do you fear talking to people about the Lord? Here's what I want you to do, nip this fear in the bud, and whatever causes you to fear more than the other, go out and do it. I'm serious—just do it! You will find it wasn't as bad as you thought it would be. And yes, you'll probably stumble a bit, and that's fine. It shows the other person you're human. I'm telling you, Holy Spirit will be with you and walk you through every step of the way.

Questions to Ponder and Answer for Chapter 11: The Church Is Breaking Out!

1. What is one of the main ingredients in this tsunami wave of healing glory?

    _____

    _____

    _____

2. Give two reasons why there has been such great loss of members in the established Church?

    _____

    _____

    _____

3. Why should you love as the Father loves?

    _____

    _____

_____

4. What is the fast and furious (fifth wave) against?

_____

_____

_____

5. The sixth wave, the tsunami wave of healing glory cannot be what?

_____

_____

_____

6. How do we reach the multitudes?

_____

_____

_____

7. From where is the Church breaking out?

_____

_____

_____

8. God uses what type of people?

_____

_____

_____

9. What is God not seeking in you?

_____

_____

_____

10. What qualifies you to be used by God?

_____

_____

11. What are the fourth and fifth key points about hands-on teaching?

_____

_____

_____

12. What can you do if you don't like the condition of your heart toward God?

_____

_____

_____

Personal Assessment

Is there a resurgence of resurrection power taking place within me during these trying times? Am I being controlled by a religious spirit? Or am I in bondage to the ways of this world? Am I allowing this great healing force to work within me to reach out to those around me? Do I know my arena of influence? Or am I still working on figuring this out? Am I sold out for Messiah? Or do I need to repent of some sins and make necessary changes in my life?

Group Discussion

Talk about general things that need to be repented for and discuss necessary changes in lifestyle that will help curb sinful desires. Discuss the seven key points that I mention in regard to hands-on-training with Holy Spirit. Can you pinpoint where you are in this process?

Appendix

Answers for Chapter Questions

Answers for Chapter 1:
A Tsunami Wave of Healing Glory

1. With a great earthquake.

2. Matthew 28:2.

3. First, a wave of worship. Then comes the wave of repentance. Afterward, a wave of revelation truth found only in the Word of God. In the midst of these incoming waves rushes in a wave of the baptism of Holy Spirit with the evidence of praying in tongues. Then comes a fast and furious wave against the spirit of death. Then a most powerful wave of healing glory that cannot be stopped.

4. Because it is an example of what is happening around the world, whether we are inside or outside, in a conference, or out on the street. Wherever God's people are, this tsunami wave of healing glory is breaking forth.

5. He wants to use you for His glory.

6. The urgency of the times we are living in.

7. I should care more about the eternal well-being of people who are not in right standing with Jesus than I care about myself, because I know I am eternally saved.

Answers for Chapter 2:
A Life-Expression of Worship

1. An expression of worship to the Most High God.

2. Worship Him in spirit and in truth.

3. Worship is a reflection of what is stored up in the heart for our Lord.

4. This type of worship is loud, spontaneous, joyful, and filled with acts of worship—dance.

5. By taking a stand of faith against evil. Pledging allegiance to God. Not giving in to the spirit of fear. Trusting God with my life. Declaring words of faith. And acting on my words of faith.

6. A priest is someone who approaches God on behalf of others. A priest is an intercessor.

7. I have been given authority to rule and reign over satan and all of his wicked works (see Luke 10:19), and with this same authority believers can subdue the earth and have dominion over it (see Genesis 1:26-29).

8. With my heart.

9. People are built up by the Scriptures, ministered to in the realm of the prophetic, delivered from the heaviness of the world, healed, and made whole in spirit, soul (mind and emotions) and in their physical bodies.

10. Continuously.

11. To bless and to kneel.

12. Into my daily life.

13. "Therefore, whether you eat or drink, or whatever you do, do all to the glory of God" (1 Corinthians 10:31).

Answers for Chapter 3:
Plunge into the Deep Waters of Repentance

1. Sanctify the Church.

2. Our eternal relationship with the Lord.

3. Personal access into every area of our lives.

4. The sin of entitlement is rampant in the earth today. These are the people, including Christians, who whine and complain about everything. Their thoughts and words are negative. They are impatient and demanding and think everyone owes them everything for nothing. They seem to get nowhere in life.

5. Pray for forgiveness. Turn away from selfishness. Look for ways to meet the needs of others. Don't think of yourself greater than you really are. Appreciate the gifts and talents of others. Do what you do for God's glory, not your own.

6. Turn from wicked ways.

7. He will hear from Heaven and forgive our sin and heal our land.

8. Speak up and take action against spiritual rats of racism.

9. In the name of the Lord and with love.

10. His love.

11. With very unique traits.

12. As equals.

13. Free will, salvation, and faith to believe.

14. According to Strong's G96, the Greek word is adokimos; it means not standing the test, or not approved. It also means what does not prove itself such as it ought, unfit, unproved, or rejected.

15. Read God's Word daily. Think about what you've read throughout the day. Ask Holy Spirit how to apply your reading to your life.

16. The Lord will hear when they call to Him.

Answers for Chapter 4:
How to Escape to Higher Ground

1. "Get ready for the coming of the Lord is at hand."
2. Intercession.
3. Elevate its power to a higher level of expectation.
4. Deactivate mediocre faith and raise to a new level of unparalleled faith.
5. We wrestle against principalities, against powers, against the rulers of the darkness of this age, against spiritual hosts of wickedness in the heavenly places.
6. The enemy's heart burns with hatred for us. He knows that his time to steal, kill and destroy us is short.
7. Use the all-powerful name of Jesus on the offense—attack the enemy first.
8. Because he is a lying spirit, fearful of the truth, and what will happen when God's truth is revealed to us.

Answers for Chapter 5:
God Expects Us to Preach the Truth

1. An evangelist.
2. Preach it.
3. In season and out of season.
4. Turn away from the truth.
5. Listen to someone who actually believes what they are saying, and puts action behind their words.
6. Rebuke the action and avoid unnecessary insults.
7. To encourage or admonish someone to do something.
8. The topic of being told we are to endure afflictions.

9. No. The thief.

10. Give an account to others about our faith in the Lord.

11. An ambassador for Christ.

Answers for Chapter 6:
The Last Days Harvest

1. He rages war against it.

2. Because he wants to steal, kill, and destroy.

3. It's great; the laborers are few; pray that the Lord of the harvest will send out laborers.

4. They are spiritually hungry for the Lord and angry with God and those who profess to believe in Him.

5. Hope.

6. To be among a Body that's weak in faith.

7. Come from a heart of love for Him, toward them.

8. As a healer on this earth.

9. Signs and wonders.

10. Read my Bible again. Pay attention to what I listen to. Guard what I watch on television. Choose friends of faith.

11. An evangelistic tool.

12. No.

13. By hearing and hearing the word of God.

14. To go out and win the lost with amazing signs and wonders

15. Brand-new converts.

16. Unchurched.

17. A religious spirit.

18. Jesus.

19. To be accepted and loved into the real family of God.

20. Start with prayer and ask Holy Spirit for His plan for your role in the end time harvest.

Answers for Chapter 7:
Revive and Come Alive Again

1. Because they lost their first love.
2. The persecuted church.
3. The church of Pergamum.
4. Idol worship, false gods, false teachings, and acts of immorality.
5. The church of Thyatira.
6. The church of Sardis.
7. Because of her faithfulness to God.
8. Lukewarm.
9. The heart.
10. Living off the backs of past spiritual greats.
11. The deadbeat Christian.
12. The Living God.
13. The heart of God.
14. Holy Spirit.
15. Rivers of living water.
16. "Not by might nor by power, but by My Spirit."
17. Divisions.
18. Go to our room, shut the door and pray to the Father in secret.

Answers for Chapter 8:
The Healing Power of God's Love

1. A loveless society.
2. A father figure.
3. A heart toward his family.

4. Love and seduction.

5. When they belong to something good, (a healthy family unit and church) and that their safety is valued.

6. Because we live in a fallen world.

7. Satan, the thief.

8. The unconditional love of God and the power of His love found within the pages of His Word—the Holy Bible.

9. The weak and the vulnerable.

10. The love of Jesus Christ.

11. To release the healing power of the Lord into desperately needy people today.

Answers for Chapter 9:
We Cannot Remain Silent!

1. If the Church kept silent.

2. The pressure of persecution.

3. The fear of financial loss.

4. Jesus Christ or the spirit of mammon.

5. Our spiritual legal rights.

6. Authority over satan and all of his wicked works.

7. Second Chronicles 7:14.

Answers for Chapter 10:
Surrendering Our Weakness and Strength to Him

1. To surrender and hand over my strength to God.

2. "Some trust in chariots and some in horses, but we will remember and trust in the name of the Lord our God."

3. The latest in this world's technology.

4. Human speed and strength.

5.   That God uses only very gifted people to do great tasks for Him.

6.   God's greatness within me.

7.   The flow of God's anointing in my life.

8.   May be hard to humble myself before God, admit I'm prideful, and forget that it's His greatness in me that causes the miraculous intervention of God to manifest in my life.

9.   That my gifts and talents, wisdom and strength are not humanly conceived, but God-given.

10. I can magnify the problems I'm facing.

11. Or I can glorify the power of the Lord's provision.

Answers Chapter 11:
The Church Is Breaking Out!

1.   The resurgence of resurrection power in believers.

2.   Because of a religious spirit and the pull of the ways of the world.

3.   To release the resurrection power of life.

4.   A spirit of death.

5.   Stopped.

6.   With a great healing force. By living out our calling in our arena of influence; everyone has the opportunity they need to hear the Good News of salvation.

7.   From the four walls of our gathering places.

8.   Ordinary people.

9.   Titles, seminary degrees, or extensive ministry exposure.

10. A willing heart surrendered after Him.

11. Believe His Word as the undeniable truth, and step out of your comfort zone.

12. Repent and make the necessary changes to be sold out for the Messiah in these troubling times—and in all times.

About the Author

Becky is a dynamic preacher of the Gospel, healing evangelist, prophetess to the nations, Destiny Image author, and host of the powerful teaching program, *Empowered for Healing and Miracles*, featured globally on the It's Supernatural! Network on ISN and conducts healing services, seminars, and conferences globally.

Becky spent twenty-five years in the trenches of service for Jesus Christ in an orphanage in Guatemala, Central America. God performed many miracles through Becky during that time, including the raising of the dead. Now the Lord is releasing Becky to equip the Body of Christ in the earth realm on a much greater scale.

Her and her husband, David, celebrate forty-one years of marriage, have eight children, three adult biological and five adopted, one son-in-law, four daughters-in-law and twelve grandchildren, and live in Arizona, U.S.A.